VIRTUAL
WAR

Kosovo and beyond

Michael Ignatieff

Chatto & Windus
LONDON

Published by Chatto & Windus 2000

1 3 5 7 9 10 8 6 4 2

Portions of some of these chapters appeared in different form in the following: 'Improvising on the Brink'
as 'The Dream of Albanians' in *The New Yorker*, January 11, 1999; 'Balkan Physics' in *The New Yorker*, May
10, 1999; 'The Virtual Commander' in *The New Yorker*, August 2, 1999; 'Justice and Revenge' as 'The
Trials of Louise Arbour' in *Saturday Night Magazine*, October, 1999; 'The War of Words: a Dialogue on
Intervention' as 'Is military intervention over Kosovo justified?' in *Prospect*, June 1999.

First published in Great Britain in 2000 by
Chatto & Windus
Random House, 20 Vauxhall Bridge Road,
London SW1V 2SA

Random House Australia (Pty) Limited
20 Alfred Street, Milsons Point, Sydney,
New South Wales 2061, Australia

Random House New Zealand Limited
18 Poland Road, Glenfield,
Auckland 10, New Zealand

Random House (Pty) Limited
Endulini, 5A Jubilee Road, Parktown 2193, South Africa

The Random House Group Limited Reg. No. 954009

A CIP catalogue record for this book
is available from the British Library

Papers used by Random House are natural,
recyclable products made from wood grown in sustainable forests.
The manufacturing processes conform to the environmental
regulations of the country of origin

ISBN 0-7011-69435

Typeset by SX Composing DTP, Rayleigh, Essex
Printed and bound in Great Britain by Biddles Ltd, Guildford

Contents

VIRTUAL WAR

ALSO BY MICHAEL IGNATIEFF

Asya

Scar Tissue

Blood and Belongings: Journeys into the New Nationalism

The Russian Album

The Needs of Strangers

A Just Measure of Pain

The Warrior's Honor: Ethnic War and the Modern Conscience

Isaiah Berlin: A Life

INTRODUCTION

Kosovo, April 3, 1999: NATO pictures from a camera on the missile
itself, hitting a target. Urosevac Army Center.
(Photo © 6206/GAMMA)

Introduction

'This was not, strictly speaking, a war.'
General Wesley K. Clark, September 16, 1999.[1]

The Kosovo conflict looked and sounded like a war: jets took off, buildings were destroyed and people died. For the civilians and soldiers killed in air strikes and the Kosovar Albanians murdered by Serbian police and paramilitaries the war was as real – and as fraught with horror – as war can be.

For the citizens of the NATO countries, on the other hand, the war was virtual. They were mobilized, not as combatants but as spectators. The war was a spectacle: it aroused emotions in the intense but shallow way that sports do. The events in question were as remote from their essential concerns as a football game, and even though the game was in deadly earnest, the deaths were mostly hidden, and above all, they were someone else's. If war becomes unreal to the citizens of modern democracies, will they care enough to restrain and control the violence exercised in their name?

Will they do so, if they and their sons and daughters are spared the hazards of combat? Although the war galvanized opinion across the planet, the number of people who actually went to war was small: 1500 members of the NATO air-crews and thirty thousand technicians, support staff and offices at headquarters. On the opposite side were the air-defense specialists of Serbia, numbering less than a thousand, and forty thousand soldiers, dug into redoubts and bunkers in Kosovo and Serbia. Face to face combat occurred rarely and then only between KLA guerillas and Serbian forces on the Kosovo-Albanian order. For NATO combatants the experience of war was less visceral than calculative, a set of split-second decisions made through the lens of a gun camera or over a video-conferencing system. Those who struck from the air seldom saw those they killed.

It was also a virtual war in a political and legal sense. It did not receive explicit sanction either from the United Nations or from the legislatures of the nations who went to war. It was prosecuted in an ambiguous legal state and it achieved a 'military technical agreement', which decided nothing but the detail of NATO's unopposed entry into Kosovo and left open the future status of the very territory over which the war was fought. The result suggests that if we won a victory, it too was virtual.

It was the kind of war fought by peoples who have known fifty years of peace; the kind of war a nation fights when it wants to, not when it must, when values rather than survival are on the line; when commitment is intense but also shallow.

What is new here? The contrast with the Gulf War, only eight years before, is instructive. Since that war employed recently developed precision weapons, especially Cruise missiles, it was heralded at the time as the first of a new age of wars. In retrospect it was the last of the old wars: it mobilized a huge land force and the vast logistical support required to sustain it, and it was fought for a classic end, to reverse a straightforward case of territorial aggression against a member state of the United Nations. Soldiers were committed in full expectation of casualties.

Kosovo broke new ground. It was a war fought for a new end: the defense of a party to a civil war within a state. It was fought without ground troops, in the hope and expectation that there would be no casualties at all. And so it proved. Technological mastery removed death from our experience of war. But war without death – to our side – is war that ceases to be fully real to us: virtual war.

What was new about the Kosovo war, therefore, was the impunity with which it was waged. But if impunity is required before values are defended, what exactly are values worth? This is the first question and the second is: If Western nations can employ violence with impunity, will they not be tempted to use it more often? The answers to these questions are not obvious. For the future depends not on us alone but on our enemies. They, like us, are drawing their own conclusions from the way we seek to avoid the mortal hazard of war.

My experience of the Kosovo war began in December 1998 in Pristina and Belgrade, observing American attempts to broker a diplomatic solution to the crisis. In April 1999, I was in the refugee camps in Macedonia, observing the deportation of the Kosovar nation. Later, I was at NATO military headquarters in

Belgium, watching the commanders improvise an air war without a ground component. In late June I followed NATO forces into the ruined towns of Kosovo. Next month, I was in the small villages on the road between Prizren and Djakovica where war crimes investigators were digging up mass graves. Finally, I visited Belgrade and the friends of mine who had become enemies.

Five characters figure prominently in my narrative of the war and its aftermath: Richard Holbrooke, architect of American diplomacy in the Balkans; Wesley Clark, Supreme Allied Commander, Europe; Louise Arbour, prosecutor of the War Crimes Tribunal; Robert Skidelsky, British peer and critic of the war; and finally, Aleksa Djilas, Yugoslav opponent of the bombing campaign. My encounters with these figures, especially the opponents of the war, put my own convictions to the test. I supported the military intervention, but as I defended my views, I came to realize the extent to which all exercises in political judgment depend on the creation of 'virtual realities', abstractions that simplify causes and consequences. War is the easiest of realities to abstract in this way, and the language of human rights provides a powerful new rhetoric of abstract justification. Keeping control of war in the modern age means keeping control of this powerful new rhetoric, making sure that the cause of human rights does not lure citizens into wars that end up abusing the very rights they were supposed to defend.

Just as we can do too much in the name of human rights, we can also do too little. Doing too little was the theme of two previous books – *Blood and Belonging* and *The Warrior's Honor* – about ethnic nationalism and ethnic war[2]. This book has become the third in a trilogy that I never intended to write and that has assumed a shape I never foresaw. An essential theme in all three has been a critique of the way Western governments have used military power to protect human rights since the end of the Cold War. In 1993 American troops intervened to deliver food and create order in Somalia, but they departed when 18 Americans were killed in a fire-fight. In 1994 in Rwanda, UN peace-keepers evacuated foreign nationals when the Hutu government began its genocidal program but stood by helpless, unable to prevent the murder of nearly a million Tutsis. Finally, in July 1995, the Dutch government sent in peace-keepers to protect the civilians of Srebrenica but instead its troops delivered them up to execution and deportation by the Serbs. These terrible events leave the UN entering the next millennium with the credibility of its contingents in ruins. The common theme in these failures was the inability of governments to back principle with decisive military force. Despite our apparent victory, this theme is also at the center of the Kosovo story: why nations that have never been more immune from the risks of waging war should remain so unwilling to run them.

Virtual War attempts to explain this paradox, by exploring the new technology of war and the emerging morality governing its use. Those – and I include myself – who believe in using force as a last resort in defending or protecting human rights need to understand military power much better than we usually do. If we will the ends, we had better will the right means. For the means we select may betray our ends. The aim of this book, like that of my two previous ones, is modest. I have no policy prescriptions for politicians, and no advice for generals. I am writing for citizens, so that when we are asked to go to war again, as we surely will, we will know of what we speak and will be able to act on what we know.

London, December 20, 1999

IMPROVING ON THE BRINK

Richard Holbrooke facing reporters at the Belgrade Hyatt Hotel, March 23, 1999, after failing to persuade Milosevic to accept the NATO proposals.
(AP Photo/Darko Vojinovic)

Improvising on the Brink, December 1998

Ten days before Christmas, 1998, Richard Holbrooke is strolling through the Plaka, the old street market in Athens. He is both taller and thinner than he looks in photographs, a rangy, bespectacled 57-year-old in a creased suit, pecking away at a bag of roast chestnuts bought from a street vendor, joking with the American ambassador to Greece, Nick Burns, while a wedge of Greek security men moves both men towards a taverna for a meal of *souvlaki*. He is discoursing loudly on ostracism, the ancient Athenian democratic practice by which citizens voted annually to banish the most egregiously offensive of their politicians. This practice, he seemed to be suggesting, was worth emulating. Five thousand miles away, American democracy was preparing its own version of ostracism, the impeachment of a President.

Although he is not even a US government official – he is a
private citizen, a vice-chairman of Crédit Suisse First Boston in
New York – Holbrooke shapes American policy throughout the
whole region of southern Europe which stretches south from
the Balkans, through Greece and Turkey. He owes his prestige
to his success in negotiating the Dayton Accords in 1995 which
ended the war in Bosnia. As the Administration's special envoy
for the Balkans, he also sorted out a dispute between Greece
and Macedonia which in 1995 was threatening to lead to war.
He is also special envoy for Cyprus, and has just flown in from
Istanbul where he spent a weekend trying to edge Greeks and
Turks a centimetre closer to resolving the deadlock which has
divided the island for twenty-five years. And this autumn,
Holbrooke has been given the most challenging task of all, to
oversee United States policy in Kosovo, an impoverished
southern province of Yugoslavia, where predominantly Muslim
ethnic Albanians outnumber the Serbs who govern them by a
ratio of ten to one, and where an armed insurrection, led by the
Kosovo Liberation Army, has been growing steadily since it
began, two years before.

When Yugoslavia was ruled by Marshal Tito, Kosovo had been
a self-governing province of Serbia, and Kosovars had enjoyed
substantial autonomy. In the late 1980s, the Serbs in the
province began to protest at their discrimination at the hands of
Kosovar authorities. When Milosevic took power in Serbia he
seized on these grievances and began to build his power base as
defender of Serbian minorities throughout Yugoslavia, but
especially in Kosovo. In 1989, Milosevic abolished Kosovar
autonomy, re-asserted Serbian direct rule and purged Kosovars
from jobs in government and education. Kosovars responded

with a boycott of Serbian institutions and a non-violent campaign, led by their leader Ibrahim Rugova, that aimed at creating a parallel network of schools, health-care centers and municipal government run by the Kosovars themselves. The Serb authorities tried to stem the Kosovar movement with arrests, detention and harassment. Until the Dayton accord of 1995, Kosovars kept their struggle non-violent, hoping to attract Western support. But when the Dayton accords failed to make any mention of their grievances, young Kosovars, especially those who had gone into emigration abroad, began to plan for an uprising.

It was among émigré Kosovars in the guest-worker communities of Germany, Switzerland, Italy and France that a small group, calling themselves the Kosovo Liberation Army, began to gather arms and prepare for a hit and run campaign directed against Serbian police and military installations in Kosovo. Operating from bases inside neighboring Albania, the KLA, at first a small band of poorly trained and amateurish gunmen, started killing Serb policemen, postmen and government officials. The Serb military police – the MUP – counter-attacked with reprisals directed at villages which gave shelter to the KLA guerillas. In late February 1998, one such reprisal killed 80 civilians, in the Drenica region of central Kosovo. This massacre sent shock-waves throughout Kosovo: it marked the end of the campaign of non-violent resistance and the onset of mass armed struggle. Hoping to exploit this tide of local support, the KLA launched an offensive which by July had seized up to one third of the country. But in late July they over-reached themselves, taking Orahovac, a town too large for them to hold. Milosevic launched a counter-attack, and in the Serbian offensive which followed, villages were rocketed, two hundred thousand civilians were driven from their homes into the mountains, and the KLA were driven back to the areas bordering Albania. Throughout the summer of 1998, the international community issued condemnations of the Milosevic counter-offensive, but it became clear that many Western governments were quietly doing nothing, waiting for it to succeed.

After the massacres by Serb police and troops in the Drenica valley in September, Holbrooke went to Belgrade to compel Milosevic to 'internationalize' the Kosovo problem, that is, to accept that it was no longer a strictly internal matter. Milosevic refused. It took an Act Ord, an order from NATO headquarters, authorizing the bombing of Yugoslav installations to make him give ground. To show that he meant business, Holbrooke got most American embassy personnel evacuated to Hungary; sensitive files were shredded and hard-drives were destroyed. All the while Holbrooke pressed Milosevic to give in. At the last moment, Milosevic relented and allowed the deployment in Kosovo of a Verification Mission of unarmed monitors.

The body controlling the monitors is the 54-nation Organization for Security and Cooperation in Europe. Based in Vienna the OSCE is a European outfit but it is also part of the American-made tool-kit for the region and the monitors in Kosovo are under the command of William Walker, a veteran American diplomat. The purpose of the Verification Mission is to ensure that the Yugoslav army stay in barracks and the Kosovar guerillas stay up in the mountains. Simultaneously, Milosevic committed himself to negotiate with the Kosovars about the future of the province. He is adamant that it remains part of Yugoslavia; the Kosovars are equally determined to fight for independence.

The man who is trying to bridge this apparently impossible

gap is not Holbrooke himself, but a bespectacled, sandy-haired and determined American, Chris Hill, the United States special envoy for Kosovo. By air or by motorcade, he shuttles between Pristina and Belgrade carrying proposals designed to give the Kosovars limited autonomy, but sidestepping the question of independence. So far, neither side is prepared to accept this compromise.

Now it is December and the winter has frozen the combatants in place. The guerillas now control most of the mountains, villages and forest paths and have the tacit or active support of most of the ethnic Albanian population. Serb tanks and armored vehicles control the asphalt roads, the capital Pristina and not much else. In the spring, everyone expects the fighting to begin again.

Holbrooke has flown back into the region to check with Hill on the state of the negotiations, to talk to Bill Walker in Pristina about the deployment of the monitors, to verify whether the tense ceasefire between the KLA guerillas and the Yugoslav forces in Kosovo is holding and, last but not least, to see Milosevic again. The meeting is at Holbrooke's initiative: he's in the region and he wants to use the opportunity to keep the lines open.

After four years of direct negotiations, Holbrooke probably knows Milosevic better than anyone except Milosevic's notorious wife. But their meetings are becoming steadily more controversial back home. American senators are asking out loud whether in negotiating with Milosevic, Holbrooke isn't lending legitimacy to a ruthless authoritarian. Even James Rubin, spokesman for Secretary of State Madeleine Albright, distanced the State Department from the Holbrooke approach, in a briefing at the beginning of December: 'Milosevic has been at the center of every crisis in the former Yugoslavia over the last decade. He is not simply part of the problem; Milosevic *is* the problem.' When I asked Holbrooke about the Rubin briefing he rolled his eyes. The administration, and particularly Albright, he said, had to avoid seeming to be cozy with Milosevic. Yet there was no realistic prospect of overthrowing his regime. Holbrooke was adamant: the path to peace in the Balkans has to pass through Milosevic's office.

While strolling up the crowded market street in Athens, looking for jewelry for his wife, Holbrooke is also waiting Milosevic's call. The proposed meeting is on again, off again. I have been invited along by Holbrooke to watch American diplomacy in action, at a time when a president is facing impeachment, his Middle East peace initiative is foundering, and Cruise missiles are being readied for a strike against Iraq. In these circumstances, Kosovo has slipped down the agenda. What coherence American policy in the Balkans still possesses is down to Holbrooke. He is an intuitive, sometimes impulsive negotiator but he clearly wants to be seen as a grand strategist in the Kissinger mode, if not in the same vein. He sees himself as more of a liberal moralist than Kissinger, and this is hardly surprising as Kissinger has been scathing about American attempts to hold together a multi-ethnic Bosnia, doubting whether America should waste its power intervening in civil wars and humanitarian catastrophes. Holbrooke wants to demonstrate that his success at Dayton marked a watershed in the use of American power, not just in this region, but in the world. It showed the tired Europeans and dispirited UN that American leadership could stop civil war and impose a peace, even if it included de facto ethnic partition. Dayton proved what America can accomplish when it uses ruthless means – air strikes or the threat of them, round the clock negotiations and the immense force of Presidential authority – to achieve peace.

In Kosovo, Holbrooke wants America to end the moral defeatism which seized hold of Europe and the UN and which led to the catastrophe of Srebrenica, when Bosnia Muslims were massacred in full sight of UN troops in July 1995. He wants in Kosovo, to show that his own highly personalized diplomacy can still achieve results. So there are high stakes in play in this remote and bloody place in southern Europe.

One curious feature of this vision is how little place it accords the United Nations. Holbrooke himself is Clinton's nominee as the next American ambassador to the UN, but in his negotiations with Milosevic, the UN was not given the slightest role in the Kosovo Verification Mission. Holbrooke is both sentimental about the UN's humanitarian relief agencies and ruthlessly pragmatic about its place in American geo-strategy. Kofi Annan's organization is there, essentially, to provide Security Council authority for actions which, if they are to be effective at all, must be led by the United States.

Holbrooke rejects the Kissingerian idea of diplomacy as chess. It's more like jazz, he says, improvisation on a theme. As he wanders through the Plaka, he is already improvising, hoping to pick up a meeting with Milosevic which will take the grand design – peace through American power – one inch further. As he strolls along, Holbrooke passes an elderly male Kosovar refugee, playing a blue plastic accordion, his Yugoslav passport in the yellow cup at his feet. The accordion's wheezing melody is lost as Holbrooke's cellular phone suddenly rings. It is Chris Hill, hundreds of miles to the north in a convoy of American jeeps on the snowy roads between Pristina and Belgrade. Hill has just heard from Milosevic's office. Holbrooke snaps the cell-phone back in his pocket and tells Burns the news: the meeting with Milosevic is on for tomorrow night.

Next day, at 7:30 in the morning in the American embassy in Athens, Holbrooke comes into the dining room. His hair is wet from the shower and his tie is still unknotted. 'Heard the news?' he asks, finishing off the last segments of a mandarin orange. Thirty-one Kosovar guerillas were killed overnight by Yugoslav forces as they crossed the mountains from Albania into Kosovo. It is the most serious military incident since the agreement negotiated between Milosevic and Holbrooke in October.

Twelve hours after the border incident, and possibly in retaliation, masked gunmen burst into a bar in the town of Pec in western Kosovo and sprayed automatic weapons fire across the pool room. More than twenty people were shot and four unarmed Serb teenagers, between the ages of thirteen and eighteen, were killed. Before this incident, Kosovo guerilla fighters had struck mostly military and security targets. The Pec attack may signal an ominous change of tactics. As Holbrooke's motorcade heads for Athens airport he says, above the whining police sirens, 'We are headed into a real mess.' From the jaunty way he bounds up the stairs to his plane, he seems to relish the prospect.

Inside the US Air Force 10-seater executive jet, Holbrooke kicks off his shoes and begins studying a sheaf of faxes which arrived at the embassy overnight. 'People say I have no instructions.' (It is widely believed that he is a loose cannon.) 'Actually I have twelve pages of them.' He speaks of a loose 'collective' making policy in the Balkans: they all go by their first names, 'Sandy' Berger, the national-security advisor; 'Strobe'

Talbott, the Deputy Secretary of State, and above all, 'Madeleine' Albright. For the first time in days, he falls silent. He sips a tomato juice, underlines carefully, pursing his lips, then rips off the cover sheet on the faxes and on the back writes out a checklist for the meeting with Milosevic. The serrated peaks of Bosnia, dusted with snow, roll out below us.

Europeans talk of Holbrooke as if he were the imperial proconsul of the Balkans: the one who made the hard rain fall on Serb sites in the bombing which led to Dayton, the one who re-drew the boundaries on the maps. Yet apart from the ground troops wintering in Bosnia, the American investment in the region is small, and Holbrooke's progress through the region is not pro-consular in style. The plane heading to Belgrade is empty: he has no staff of his own and he carries his own bags. He depends on the US embassies in the region for logistical support. The execution of American policy is in the hands of a small number of dedicated but overworked State Department officials, based in Belgrade and Skopje, Macedonia, many of them, like Chris Hill, veterans of the Dayton process. Holbrooke is the unofficial coach of the team: chief motivator, psychologist, strategist, and, when top-level negotiations are required, the heavy-lifter of choice. His identification with embassy officials is strong; he was a career diplomat himself and can still remember what it was like to be a junior officer in the US embassy in Vietnam in 1962. He flatters, cajoles, berates and teases his people constantly, but I do not see the bullying and ruthlessness he has been accused of. Embassy staff appear to regard him with affectionate exasperation. Whenever he touches down, the word goes out: 'The ego has landed.' The ego is large, but it gets results.

However large Holbrooke's ego, and however large his ambitions for American power in the region, American reluctance to get sucked into the quagmire of Balkan politics remains a fundamental constraint. The Pentagon didn't want to bomb Milosevic in October and doesn't want American troops to be committed in Kosovo; most of the American public barely knows where Kosovo is; and the President and the White House are hunkered down in the trenches of a gruelling battle over impeachment.

Holbrooke is not the first American to try shaping the resistant material of the Balkans into a grander design. It was President Woodrow Wilson who first enunciated the right of national self-determination for the subject peoples of the Ottoman and Austro-Hungarian empires at the Versailles Conference in 1918; Versailles draftsmen laid out the borders which Balkan states have been fighting over ever since. Holbrooke likes to cite Harold Nicolson's *Peacemaking, 1919*, the British writer's mordant account of Woodrow Wilson's failures at Versailles. 'America, eternally protected by the Atlantic, desired to satisfy her self-righteousness while disengaging her responsibility.'

Bringing self-righteousness and responsibility into line is never easy, and it's not obvious why America should still be attempting, eighty years later, to remedy the errors of Versailles. Where does a place like Kosovo figure in American national interest?

In 1989, when Milosevic consolidated his power in Yugoslavia, he abolished the limited autonomy previously enjoyed by the Kosovars under the Tito constitution of 1974. Since then, police attempts to suppress the rising demand for Kosovar independence have grown more brutal. The Serbs claim the KLA are a terrorist threat, but many states in Europe – Britain in Northern Ireland, Spain in the Basque country –

have faced terror campaigns without having to rocket villages, or massacre citizens. That's the issue here – Serb repression has long since passed the point of legitimate self-defence. This is what gives outsiders the grounds – if not the right – to intervene in a civil war. Besides, Kosovo is too strategically placed for its troubles ever to be just an internal matter. If Kosovo exploded, other countries could well go up in flames with it. Kosovo stands in the center of a combustible region which stretches from Italy, through Greece, across the Eastern Mediterranean to the Turkish border with Iraq.

What makes the region combustible is Albania, the failed state in its midst. Always the poorest state in Europe, despite its access to the sea, Albania was further impoverished by the years of corrupt, paranoid and despotic communist rule. After the fall of Communism, a succession of democratic regimes have tried and failed to prevent the country from fragmenting into clan-dominated enclaves. In early 1997, following the collapse of a nation-wide pyramid-investment scheme, Albania disintegrated altogether. Its army disbanded and the population looted the government arsenals, making off with an estimated three million grenades and bombs and seven hundred thousand rifles. These arms quickly found their way into the hands of the Kosovo guerillas who now gather in Albania, train there, and cross the border into their homeland. This helped to trigger full-scale insurrection in February 1998. And there is no reason it should stop there. Nearby Montenegro, Macedonia and Greece also have substantial ethnic Albanian populations. Already they are funnelling arms and fighters to their borders in Kosovo and many of them dream of one day carving out a greater Albanian state, combining Kosovo and Albania with the Albanian areas of their own nations.

Underlying the Kosovo problem then, is a serious dilemma, which pits *realpolitik* against high principle; respect for state sovereignty – even rogue states like Serbia have rights – and human rights. If Kosovo is forced to remain in Yugoslavia, its people face a future of unending brutality at the hands of the Milosevic government; on the other hand, if Kosovo is granted its independence, it may destabilize the whole of NATO's southern region.

The plane is beginning to make its descent into a cold and misty Belgrade. When Holbrooke puts his papers back in his briefcase, he says he's worried that he hasn't visited Kosovo. After the KLA killings in Pec, it will look bad. The situation needs calming. As the plane halts in front of the terminal and the cars for his motorcade careen into place, Holbrooke bounds forward to the cockpit to talk to the pilot. Then he clambers down on to the tarmac to tell Richard Miles, the head of the American embassy in Belgrade, to get flight clearance to head back down to Pristina. There is just enough time, before the meeting with Milosevic, to plan a trip to Kosovo. Calls are placed to Milosevic's office. Turning the plane around is a typical Holbrooke improvisation: catching Milosevic off guard, energizing his weary team of monitors and American staff on the ground in Pristina and getting a chance to see for himself just how bad the situation is.

In the Belgrade airport VIP lounge, Ambassador Miles informs Holbrooke that the death toll at Pec has risen to six; and that fifteen Serb teenagers are still in Pristina hospital, recovering from gunshot wounds. Meanwhile, Holbrooke is busily putting a team together for this flying visit to Kosovo. Another American diplomat, William Walker arrives at the lounge to join his team. Holbrooke instructs Richard Miles to get some European representatives on board. An elegant Austrian ambassador in a loden coat (Wolfgang Petritsch, the European Union's special envoy for Kosovo) arrives, followed by a British Major-General, John Drewenkiewicz, a deputy chief of the Verification Mission. The ballet between Americans and Europeans is interesting to observe: publicly they are all smiles; privately the Americans are scathing about European feebleness of will, while the Europeans fulminate against American arrogance. In practice, each side knows it can't do without the other.

The final member of the team is Shaun Byrnes, another American, weary, shy, soft-spoken, dressed in khakis and Top-Siders. Byrnes deals directly with the guerillas, driving out into the so-called 'liberated areas', to remote farms, safe-houses, and wooded-areas. It's a dangerous assignment, but he prefers it to his last posting in Rome: 'I mean, how many cappuccinos can you drink?' When he reaches Pristina, his job is to find out who carried out the Pec attack and get the guerillas to repudiate it publicly – a tactic for preserving the truce.

While waiting to take off for Pristina, Holbrooke becomes concerned that he is getting 'too far ahead of the wagon train.' He phones the Operations Center at the State Department to let everyone know his plans have changed. Albright is in Jerusalem with the President; Talbott is in Madrid at a conference on Bosnia. Holbrooke calls them all, as if to demonstrate that, despite his reputation, he is a team player.

Once airborne, Holbrooke is briefed by Drewenkiewicz about the border incursion. Drawing a rough map on a sheet of foolscap, the general marks the spots where his verification team had found the bodies in the snowy woods near the

Albanian border. Holbrooke wants to know whether the incident was a fire-fight, an ambush or an execution. The Serbs have a reputation for executing prisoners. In this case, though, prisoners had survived and the monitors are trying to get to see them.

Less than thirty minutes later, the plane touches down at Pristina airport. Holbrooke transfers to a motorcade of orange-painted Chevrolet Suburbans with bullet-proof windows and armor-plated doors. The cars pass by Kosovo Polje, a vast plain ringed with low mountains, where the Serbian kings went down to historical defeat at the hands of the Turks in 1389. It was here that the Kosovar lands passed under Turkish Ottoman control for more than five centuries; it was here that the Serbian dream of reconquering Kosovo one day was born, a dream not realized until just before the World War I. And it was here, in 1989, that Milosevic held his infamous rally of 250,000 supporters which launched his campaign for a Greater Serbia. Kosovo, he proclaimed, was the heartland of the Serbian nation, and Serbs throughout the former Yugoslavia must come together in one great nation, by force of arms if need be. The speech at Kosovo Polje incited the Serb minorities to rise up against the Croatian state in 1991, and against the new Bosnian state the following year. Less than a decade later, Serbs have been driven out of Croatia, been defeated in Bosnia and are on the run in Kosovo. This explains why even Serbs opposed to Milosevic believe they cannot compromise. To give up Kosovo would be to admit, finally, the extent of the historical disaster which has overtaken them. Paradoxically, they unite around the man who led them into catastrophe.

Kosovo Polje, where the dream began, is a bleak expanse of corn-stubble, blown by the December winds. The motorcade passes bare market stalls, a few abandoned half-finished houses, geese washing themselves in half frozen ponds of muddy water. Kosovars stand huddling against the wind, watching the Americans pass. Flocks of black crows wheel and turn in the dirty sky. Inside the Chevrolet Suburban, Shaun Byrnes is talking about his contacts with the guerillas. He sits down with armed men committed to liberate Kosovo and tries to persuade them to back the American-led peace talks that will only give them autonomy. This doesn't sound promising. When asked about the risk of being taken hostage, he shrugs. Killing an American here would be a tactical mistake. What's more, the guerillas hold on to the illusion that America will eventually support them, because their struggle for independence is right and good. 'Our basic problem is that they think we support their goals,' one American official tells me. 'They're just not listening. They hear the music but they don't pay attention to the words.' This is at the heart of what could be seen as an evasive policy of procrastination. In ten or twenty years, American officials concede, *perhaps* the remaining Serbian population will be driven out, and Yugoslavia will be bled white by the cost of holding down an ethnic Albanian majority in permanent revolt. Then, but only then, Kosovar independence may happen. But that is in the future. For now, the prospect of a Kosovar state is simply too alarming to the Greeks, Macedonians and Montenegrins for the Americans to allow it to occur. So Shaun Byrnes has to tell the fighters in the farmhouses and on the mountain tops that they can't count on American support. And Chris Hill has to tell their political representatives to cut a deal with Milosevic. This may not be very attractive, but it is better, so the argument goes, than a bloodbath.

*

In the operations room of the Kosovo Verification Mission in Pristina, Holbrooke is briefed again on the border incursion. The pop-pop of small-arms fire is heard echoing over the roof-tops of the city. No one in the briefing room seems to pay it any attention. A British officer tells Holbrooke that the incidents occurred in the darkness between 2:00 and 6:00 a.m. in hilly and heavily wooded terrain. The monitors were on the site quickly, while the bodies were still warm. Holbrooke asks what kinds of weapons the guerillas were carrying. AK 47s and RPGs, he's told. These may have come from the looted Albanian arsenal, or from Albanians in exile in America and Europe. This too is a new dimension in the Kosovar equation: the funds and arms being funneled into the struggle from the hard-working Albanian diaspora (and yes – from their drug barons). Holbrooke knows the strength of this diaspora: Albanian taxi-drivers buttonhole him when he gets into cabs in New York and restaurateurs in the West 50's berate him for negotiating with Milosevic.

As for the attack on the Serb teenagers in Pec, the hunch among the British observers is that it is not a response to the border incident but a payback for an earlier shoot-out in which a female KLA fighter attempted to storm into the hospital in Pec to rescue a hospitalized comrade inside and was shot by Serb police in the hospital entrance. But by now angry Serbs are demonstrating in Pec against the Verification Mission; shots have been fired from a car south of town, while to the north of the city, near the Serb high school, the monitors' orange cars have been stoned. The funerals of the six teenagers will be held in the next few days, and these will be dangerous occasions.

Holbrooke asks the British officers what they would do if this was Northern Ireland. If the Kosovars are engaged in a terror campaign, no one understands counter-insurgency strategy better than the British. We would step up armed foot patrols; they say; we would sweep the area with armored vehicles. We would keep the two communities apart and, it goes without saying, we would infiltrate the terrorists. 'But we haven't this luxury here,' they add. The monitors are entirely unarmed. One officer on the team, when asked what he has to protect him, takes something from his pocket and holds it up with a wry smile. It is a Swiss army knife. If the American and European monitors are fired upon, it is only a matter of time before they will have to be extracted. Indeed NATO has already begun to position an extraction force – known as 'the dentists' – next door in Macedonia. As both sides ignore the monitors and keep up the killing, all that the Americans can do is call in the local press – Albanian and Serb – and appeal for calm. Ambassador William Walker, head of the Kosovo Mission, appeals to the Serb authorities and the KLA to avoid 'the downward spiral of retribution.'

Holbrooke's next appointment – on a day of makeshift appointments – is with two prominent Albanian editors, Blerim Shala and Veton Surroi, hearing their assessment of the Kosovar political leadership. Holbrooke spends hours with the Balkan press, using them to spread his message and to get information. He takes it for granted that public spin is integral to modern diplomacy. Besides, journalists are a key source of information. Talking to them is a reality check, a way out of what he calls 'the absurd bubble' of his shuttle diplomacy, running from motor-cade, to airport, to hotel, and back to airport.

The editors' prognosis is discouraging. Surroi, the elegantly dressed son of a former diplomat, says in his fluent American accent, that Rugova, the non-violent leader of the Kosovars, is

'Jell-o all the way through.' He has made too many compromises with the Serbs to be credible. Initiative is passing to harder men, like Adem Demaci, who spent a decade in Tito's jails for demanding Kosovar rights and who has links with the shadowy military command of the KLA. The Kosovar's taste for compromise is vanishing fast. There is already talk that the hidden Kosovar strategy is to provoke the Serbs into massacres and reprisals which would force NATO troops to intervene. The first stage in provoking a NATO intervention would be to drive out the unarmed monitors. Armed NATO troops would replace them and impose independence, or at least partition, on Milosevic. Such, at any rate, is the desperate dream.

Holbrooke may favor a robust armed deployment himself, but he knows how reluctant NATO would be to authorize one, so he does his best to close down the idea that NATO is waiting in the wings to ride to the rescue. He assures the Kosovar editors that if the monitors are driven out, there is no guarantee that NATO troops will replace them. The Kosovars will be on their own, face to face with Milosevic's tanks and helicopter gunships.

The Pristina visit is over. As Holbrooke's plane prepares for take off, a small, snub-nosed dun-green Yugoslav MiG flies past, at 100 metres, afterburner jetting out a bright orange flame. It is on its way to Pec, ten minutes' flying time away, to rattle the windows of the Kosovar population and to remind them who still rules in the air, if not on the ground. But it's also rattling the windows of Holbrooke's jet. He shrugs. This is standard Milosevic.

In the air, Holbrooke is handed 4 x 8 colour photographs of the incident on the Kosovo-Albanian border. He grimaces, looks away, then takes a clinical look. The pictures depict what Holbrooke, who has Vietnam experience, likes to call the last

Ho Chi Min Trail in Europe. The snow is calf-deep; the morning fog is still settled in the trees on the slopes. A faint path in the snow disappears among the trees. It is down this trail that the Kosovar uprising is re-supplied. Sniper rifles, water bottles, Serb dinars and grenades lie strewn about in the foreground, near the bodies. The eyes of the victims are mostly open. Some are bleeding from the mouth. The snow around them is stained. Most are wearing combat fatigues. No execution-style entry wounds or powder burns can be seen. It appears that they have walked into an ambush by Serb sharp-shooters equipped with night sights. The guerillas would have died without knowing where the firing was coming from. One is a woman, in her early twenties, with shining brown hair strewn against the snow, her eyes sightlessly staring up at the sky.

The photographs are sobering evidence of the key new fact which now has more influence over the course of events than Holbrooke and American power – the fact that young Kosovar men and women, for years committed to non-violence are now prepared to risk sudden death in the dark on a mountain trail, to make Kosovo free.

On the rest of the brief flight to Belgrade, the mood in the cabin is silent. Holbrooke pores over maps of Malicevo, the scene of other firefights between Yugoslav military police and the Kosovar guerillas. He is hoping to persuade Milosevic to agree to a demilitarization of Malicevo, but after Pec, after the killings at the border, it is not looking hopeful.

The jet touches down as dusk is falling in Belgrade. The third motorcade of the day, and the most lunatic, ensues as the cars fish-tail in and out of the lanes on the highway from the airport, with Milosevic's secret police in the forward black BMW, leaning out the windows on both sides, frantically waving the traffic off to the side of the road. Safely inside the American embassy grounds, Holbrooke wanders off into the garden, cell-phone clamped to his ear, trying to reach James Rubin, traveling with the presidential party in Israel. While he is talking to the Middle East in the garden, a large group of independent Serbian journalists is shown inside into the embassy dining room. Holbrooke and Hill go in to brief them on the Kosovo situation. The media are agitated by the attacks on the Serb teenagers in Pec. 'What are you doing to protect us?' a pert woman journalist with peroxide blonde hair wants to know. 'Are you in danger?' Holbrooke asks her ironically. The intention is to deflate the rhetoric before it gets exaggerated, and if that's the aim, it fails. By nightfall the Serbian media, both independent and official, are crying for vengeance.

After this meeting, Holbrooke steps into an alcove with the rugged, black-haired figure of Veran Matic, one of Serbia's most independent and resourceful editors. He assures Matic that at his meeting, now only forty-five minutes away, he will bring up Milosevic's recent crackdown on the independent media. But Matic really wants to know why Holbrooke is still talking to Milosevic at all: US policy should be undermining him and working with the democratic opposition. But who *is* there? Holbrooke pointedly asks Matic to name anyone in Belgrade capable of mounting a credible opposition. Matic shrugs eloquently and raises his jet-black eyebrows. If there was a local Vaclav Havel, Holbrooke tells Matic, he would be talking to him. Instead there are only discredited opposition leaders who can't stand to be in the same room with each other.

Privately, Holbrooke concedes that the Americans should have lent far more support to the opposition movements that coalesced in late 1997 and whose street demonstrations briefly unsettled the Milosevic regime. Holbrooke's wife, Kati Marton, a Hungarian-born writer, flew in to join these demonstrations. But the opportunities were squandered, and now the opposition is hopelessly divided. Still, one consequence of being regarded as the Balkan pro-consul is that you are believed to have magical influence over the local political situation. These illusions, Holbrooke does his best to dispel. He tells Matic, 'The responsibility for creating democracy in Serbia rests with you not with us.' These are phrases American diplomats have been wearily repeating since the days of Woodrow Wilson. Later one disillusioned embassy official confesses, 'We don't have much of a commitment in this region. If we did, Milosevic wouldn't be here.'

At last, Holbrooke heads in to the embassy dining room to prepare his meeting with Milosevic. Hill and Miles and a number of embassy officials help him to order the agenda: demanding that Milosevic relax his crackdown on the local media; trying to get him to hand over some Serbian war criminals from Bosnia who have taken refuge in Belgrade; pushing Milosevic to make some concessions to the Kosovar uprising before it is too late. Officials frantically try to locate the text of a ceasefire deal signed earlier in the year by the Kosovar guerillas in the Malicevo region. It can't be found in time. Holbrooke begins to fret. Half an hour before the meeting, Shaun Byrnes phones in with the news that the Kosovar guerillas are denying responsibility for the attack in Pec. Holbrooke charges out of the meeting, cell-phone to his ear, and orders Byrnes to get them to disown the attack publicly: he needs a public statement. 'Right now!' But it is too late. By the time he drives off to meet Milosevic, Holbrooke knows that he will be unable to tell the dictator that he has forced the guerillas to dissociate themselves from the latest terrorist attack.

Five and a half hours later, just before midnight, Holbrooke and Hill come through the main entrance of Belgrade's Hyatt Hotel to meet a line of waiting cameras and outstretched tape recorders. It's clear they have got nothing out of Milosevic. The Pec killings have provided him with a pretext to shut down negotiations on any issue. Upstairs, in the long corridors of the third floor, oblivious to the secret police microphones which must be in every heating duct, Holbrooke vents his frustration. 'Before we even sat down, he was on to us about those Serb teenagers. And he didn't let up all night.' He takes a call from Madeleine Albright, heading home from Jerusalem to Washington, on Air Force One. He seems grateful for the call, but when he hangs up he looks around at the spent and dispirited American staffers, heads bent, in the gloomy hallway and says, 'Jesus Christ, this is depressing.'

The day of improvisation has gone badly wrong. He picked up a meeting with Milosevic in the hope that he could push him towards a settlement with the Kosovars. Instead, the Kosovars have taken the fight to Milosevic, and the fragile architecture of the October settlement, put together only after the threat of air-strikes, is coming apart. Chris Hill, leaning against the door of his room, tie askew, face grey with exhaustion, says, before turning in for the night, 'Can you believe that we are still trying to liquidate the Ottoman Empire?'

At eight o'clock the next morning, at Belgrade airport, Holbrooke's jet is parked beside the one reserved for Chris Hill. 'Mine's bigger than yours,' Holbrooke jokes and Hill rolls his eyes. This is an old routine, and after what they have been through the night before, it is surprising that they can even muster the old jokes. Holbrooke then wanders off to the edge of the tarmac to phone Strobe Talbott in Madrid.

Hill is flying to Rome to brief the Italian Foreign Minister on his negotiations with Milosevic and Holbrooke is returning via Rome to New York to dine with UN Secretary General Kofi Annan. On the plane, they assess the state of the Kosovar leadership. The fighting has eroded the legitimacy of the few remaining non-violent Kosovar leaders like Ibrahim Rugova and the initiative is passing rapidly into the hands of a network of KLA military commands in the mountains and outlying villages. None have international experience or stature. None, Hill concludes, is 'ready for prime time,' and none is going to negotiate away their claim for freedom. There is a real risk that sooner rather than later, Hill will have no one to negotiate with on the Kosovar side.

On the face of it, Hill's task of bridging the gap between the Kosovars and the Serbs seems a good deal harder than the task that faced the Americans at Dayton. In Bosnia, war-weariness had concentrated minds on all sides. In Kosovo, the exhaustion is only on the Serbian side. The Kosovars' blood is up: they are anything but tired.

Publicly at least, Chris Hill believes the deal he carries around between Pristina and Belgrade in his battered leather briefcase is still possible. It is a complex plan proposing parallel institutions for the two communities in Kosovo, Yugoslav federal ones for the Serb minority, and new self-governing ones for the Albanian majority. The Serb police would get out of the villages and local policing and communal government would be handed over the Albanians. A Kosovar parliament in Pristina would train up some legitimate local leadership. Courts would be run by and for the Albanians and there would be separate school systems for Albanians and Serbs. Yugoslavia would retain border control, foreign affairs and ultimate territorial authority. It is a deal that gives autonomy to the Kosovars, but keeps sovereignty with the Serbs. The drafts of such an agreement are already circulating between both sides, and if the deal can be done, the Americans would lean on the Europeans to come up with some money to begin remedying the region's chronic poverty. Final status talks on the future of the province would be deferred for three years. What no American will say publicly – though it is an essential condition for any deal – is that the Americans would commit NATO to deploy an armed force, as in Bosnia, to keep the two sides apart and allow time for the Kosovars to develop their own institutions of self-government.

But such a deal seems evidently too little, too late. The fighters in the woods want independence not autonomy and they will fight for it now whether the Americans support them or not. The grand design which Holbrooke is pursuing looks like nothing so much as a strategy to buy some time. And time is fast running out. In the days following Holbrooke's visit, the badly beaten body of the Serbian mayor of the town of Kosovo Polje is found on the road in from Pristina airport; Yugoslav army tanks leave their barracks and engage in fierce firefights with guerilla units; in Pec and other towns, Serb police burst into houses and farms, beat up Kosovar Albanians and drag men off to prison. The unarmed American and European monitors observe the mounting violence but without arms they can do nothing to stop it.

When the plane lands at Rome airport, Hill leaves for his meeting with the Italians and Holbrooke runs to catch his flight to New York to dine with UN Secretary General Kofi Annan.

Of what I have witnessed in his company, he says, 'This is work in progress.' But what exactly is he progressing toward? He has committed his time, his reputation and a dedicated team of diplomats to the proposition that American leadership can bring stability to the Balkans. If there is a plan once Kosovo dissolves into warfare, he has kept it to himself. He holds to a simple gut conviction: that the Americans are the only people capable of replacing the Ottomans and Austro-Hungarians – the only people with the character required for an imperial vocation. It's a controversial sentiment. And Holbrooke's problem is that the Americans are turning out to be very reluctant imperialists indeed. If diplomacy is jazz, the improvisation has been ingenious, but the music keeps slipping out of control. Violent men are calling the tune. And in any case, right now the world's most powerful nation has its attention fixed elsewhere. The night that Holbrooke flies into New York, the first cruise missiles slam into Iraq. For the moment, Kosovo has vanished from Western attention.

December 1998.

Kosovo returned to the front pages two weeks later on January 15 when Serb paramilitary and police units entered the village of Racak in search of KLA commandos and murdered 45 civilians. Thereafter the descent into conflict was swift. On January 31, NATO authorized air-strikes against Serbia if it did not agree to talks with Kosovar leaders. These talks at the French château of Rambouillet, outside Paris, failed to produce agreement and further negotiations in Paris also ended in deadlock, with the Kosovar delegation reluctantly agreeing to American proposals for autonomy, accompanied by NATO troop deployments, and the Serbs refusing what they regarded as an ultimatum that imposed occupation by foreign troops. On March 24, after a final visit by Richard Holbrooke to Milosevic, NATO began air operations against Serbia. The war was to last for 78 days.

BALKAN PHYSICS

Elderly ethnic Albanian refugees rest on a hill overlooking the
Stankovec refugee camp, April 28, 1999.
(Photo Reuters/Hazir Reka)

Balkan Physics

A man-made escarpment of earth rising about a hundred feet afforded a view of the whole scene. It was there that people came to escape the dust, heat and confinement below. Dusk was settling and light was draining from the Macedonian sky. Kosovo lay five miles away, over some bare hills and from that direction you could hear muffled detonations and explosions. A convoy of NATO armored personnel carriers was visible on the skyline, green metal moving amongst the scrub pines. The most serious war in Europe since 1945 was close by, and yet it remained a ghostly presence, the bombers audible yet invisible in the fading sky. Oblivious to everything, a young couple sat on the escarpment, leaning against each other wordlessly.

Twenty-four hours before, in the abandoned ammunition dump below them, there had been no one there at all. Now there were close to eight thousand people in a tent city and thirty thousand more at an abandoned airfield within sight. Chinook helicopters wheeled in the sky, with cargo nets full of tents and ready-meals swaying from their underbellies. As they landed on the hillside behind, swarms of children ran forward and vanished into the dust clouds kicked up by the rotors. At the bottom of the escarpment women and children with plastic bottles queued for the standpipes, and a huge line – like a dun-colored python – wound right through the camp, more than five hundred yards from end to end, to the spot where French paratroopers in red berets and T-shirts were hauling ready-meals in bright yellow plastic covers out of cardboard boxes. A secondary line was already forming for the empty boxes – to use as flooring for the tents. Rain-clouds were gathering and when the rain fell, this place would turn into a quagmire.

The constituent elements of a whole nation were visible below: country-women in the flowing trousers known as *shallvare*; old men in suits wearing the conical hat known as a *qeleshe*, and then urban dwellers in tracksuits and T-shirts, architects, doctors, lawyers and professors of Pristina, Kosovo's capital, only fifty kilometers up the road. The country people were stoical and sat cross-legged on blankets, poking at the strange American ready-meals in their tin-foil packs; the city people seemed more stunned, wandering to and fro, hands to their faces, trying to take the measure of their dispossession.

The television reporters persisted in calling this place, Stankovec 2, a refugee camp and describing its inhabitants as the victims of a humanitarian disaster. But the people were not refugees but deportees: the victims of a political crime, the largest single eviction of a civilian population in Europe since 1945. The Milosevic regime in Serbia had already earned its place in the annals of political science for pioneering officially deniable ethnic cleansing in Bosnia; now Milosevic had per-fected a new weapon of war: the use of refugee flows to destabilize neighboring countries, to immobilize the logistics of NATO forces by handing them a humanitarian catastrophe, then keeping them off-balance by turning on and off the flow of refugees at the border and finally – following the adage that a guerilla swims in the local population like a fish in the sea – by draining the sea, exposing the guerillas, the Kosovo Liberation Army, who were left behind so that they could be finished off. Five weeks ago, the US bombing raids had begun. Faced with war from the air, he decided to finish his war on the Kosovars, and now a million men, women and children were fleeing for their lives. NATO's war provided perfect cover for his war. When interviewed on Serbian television, he denied having anything to do with the expulsion of the Albanians. The Kosovars, like the birds, he said, were fleeing the NATO bombs.

In quiet voices, as if still wondering at the biblical scale of it, members of a deported nation told their stories. It was clear the operation was not an explosion of local Serbian rage at the bombing, but a concerted government campaign, initiated earlier. The refugees emphasized the preparations, which seemed to have preceded the NATO air-strikes by weeks: how they knew what was coming from rumors among the Serbian population and the increasing numbers of armed men in the streets. They told of sleeping in their clothes for days before the police came, sure of their fate but helpless to avoid it since those who resisted were shot in the streets in front of their houses; of being warned by Serb neighbors who then painted *Srpska kuca* – Serb house – on their own doorways so that the marauding police and military would pass them by; of the paramilitaries in ski-masks who thundered on their doors with their rifle butts;

who gave them ten minutes to pack, so that they forgot even to take their photos or address books; how corridors of armed police lined the roads, funneling cars towards the borders, and driving those on foot – with kicks and blows – to the Pristina train station where they were loaded on to trains bound for the frontier. As they fled for their lives, the men with guns taunted them: 'Go to NATO! They will protect you!' When asked if it was the NATO bombardment which had made them flee, they were vehement: No, it was not so. They supported the bombardment. But why, they asked, weren't more bombs falling on the men who had driven them from their homes?

Their experiences left them pondering the dark complexities of people they once called friends: when a Serb came to warn them to leave, was he acting out of complicity or friendship? When he offered to keep their apartment safe, was he doing so from fraternity or greed? When Serbs leaned on their windowsills and silently watched them go, did their eyes register fear or approval? There were no such ambiguities in the brutality of the men in ski-masks, some of whose voices they recognized as one-time colleagues and former friends. When the women recalled being strip-searched and manhandled and having their family savings – wads of German marks – ripped from their undergarments, their faces would crumple into tears that expressed anger and shame but also baffled disillusion. How could human beings do this to us? Below the escarpment lay a nation in pieces, only its elementary particles, the nuclear family, still functioning. Lines of shoes were already ranged in order by the entrance of the tents; on the sloping sides of canvas, the first laundry of exile; before nightfall each tent had a small cardboard sign announcing the name of the family inside. The truly desperate were those who had been forced to leave alone and who now wandered up and down the rows of tents searching for their kin. If they saw you had a mobile phone, they came up at once with small scraps of paper with long dialing codes, begging to make just one quick call.

This need to know – to discover who had escaped, who had managed to get to Germany, who was still trapped in Kosovo – was as fundamental a need as food, shelter, water or sanitation. The French paratroopers who built the camp had provided for basic needs but not this one. To fill the gap, a heroic trio of telecommunications workers from Pau in southwestern France who called themselves *Télécoms Sans Frontières*, set up shop in a tent with a single satellite telephone. They seemed the only aid workers to grasp that the Albanians did not conform to the clichés of destitution lodged in our minds by Ethiopia or the Sudan. These people were modern Europeans, with relatives and friends in every city on the continent and they needed phones to activate these networks abroad. Soon the line for the phones was as long as the line for water.

The cellular phone also changed the experience of being at war, abolished the traditional silence between sides, making enmity more painful. Up on the escarpment, you could dial Belgrade and describe the refugees below to old friends now in enemy territory. If this was announced as a war between value systems – between ethnic cleansing and human rights, between nationalism and moral universalism – the uncomfortable truth was that many people on the other side shared the same values. They had taken to the streets in the great anti-Milosevic demonstration first in 1991 and then again in 1997, had worked for a free press, needed no instruction in what an open society was, or what democracy was, and now felt Serbian loyalties and European values beginning to sunder and split apart. They had never understood why Western governments had not done more to support democracy in Serbia, and you could not help agreeing that this had been a central policy failure of the West. But now they felt that they were being punished and bombed for the criminality of their regime and that their whole nation was under sentence of moral excommunication.

They had all seen the footage on CNN, but I told them that the deportation of the Kosovars was worse than those images, not because of the conditions – which were better than many camps in Africa – but because the ethnic cleansing had been more malign and meticulous than they could have imagined. I found myself telling another Serb friend on the phone that I did not believe in collective guilt. To hold a people responsible for the crimes of their leaders was to succumb to the ethnic determinism of the regime itself. But what I was witnessing in the camps was a crime that had to be stopped. My friend listened in chilly silence. Another friend told me, after I had described the refugee camp, that her four-year-old daughter walked around the flat in Belgrade with her stereo-earphones clamped on her ears to block out the sounds of fire-engines and sirens. I sensed that the little girl's courageous mother was the same: hardly able to bear what I was telling her.

There was a cold clarity to be found on the hillside above the camp in Macedonia, as if I had reached the end of a terrible story and understood it at last. I had lived in Belgrade for two years as a child, in the late Fifties. I once spoke Serbo-Croatian, as the language of Yugoslavia was then called. I had covered the conflict since the autumn of 1991 when Yugoslav warships shelled the old walled city of Dubrovnik in order to prevent Croatia from seceding and US warships in the Adriatic cruised nearby, watching it happen. In 1992, I had traveled through the mile upon mile of ethnically cleansed towns in the plain between Zagreb and Belgrade, left desolate by Milosevic's further attempts to prevent Croatian independence. I had been to Vukovar, that ancient Episcopal town on the Danube, between Croatia and Serbia, reduced to rubble by Serbian artillery, its rat-infested ruins patroled by Serbian paramilitary thugs who threatened to kill me if I wasn't gone by nightfall.

Three years later, I drove through central Bosnia, past the toppled minarets, gutted towns and the downed bridge at Mostar that I had crossed as a child when Yugoslavia was Tito's. Reaching Tuzla, I listened to the widows of the Srebrenica massacre, telling how they had stumbled through the minefields and across streams, carrying children crazed with fear, leaving behind the bodies of as many as seven thousand men, massacred by Ratko Mladic's Bosnian Serbs. In the following years, in Belgrade hostels and cheap hotels, I interviewed the forgotten victims of Milosevic's wars: the Serb families – more than 200,000 of them – driven out of Croatia in revenge. In the summer of 1996 I had sat with friends in Sarajevo cafés and watched them beginning to stretch, breathe and laugh after three years of brutal Serbian siege. And now, sitting on that hillside in Macedonia, watching a dispossessed nation settle in for its first nights of exile, the full measure of what had happened in the past eight years – more than a quarter of a million people killed, another two million driven from their homes – suddenly seemed insupportable. Only one thought seemed possible: this cannot go on. This must be stopped. Now. By persistent and precise military force. The claim that there was no national interest at stake here suddenly seemed offensively beside the point. Both values and interests were at stake; we had taken far too long to realize it, and these people now settling in for the night in the camps below had paid the price.

And the questions were suddenly very clear too. How was it that after eight years of repeating that we wanted to banish ethnic cleansing from Europe, we could wake up to a whole nation expelled before our eyes? How had we so misjudged Milosevic? What had to be understood was the whole dynamic of American imperial power in this region. What had been the strategy for the Balkans? Was there one? Had the United States ever understood the tragic game it was playing?

In search of answers, I went to lunch at the American embassy in Skopje, Macedonia with Ambassador Chris Hill. The embassy itself had become one of the earliest targets of the war. On March 25th, the evening after the NATO bombing campaign began, a crowd of about two thousand Macedonian Serbs swept aside the metal barriers erected by the police guarding the grounds, smashed up the satellite trucks of the foreign television companies in the parking lot and stormed over the security fence. A determined few used a flag-pole as a battering ram to attack the bullet-proof glass entrance to one of the buildings inside the compound. They withdrew under clouds of tear gas, having failed to penetrate the building. Now two weeks later, the embassy was a Fort Apache in the south Balkans, guarded by the United States Marines.

At lunchtime, the embassy canteen was serving hamburgers to huge American infantrymen in body armor, their M-16 rifles racked up against the walls, gun butts wedged between rows of Kevlar helmets. Sitting in their midst was Chris Hill, eating Macedonian salad, and looking as out of place as a college professor in a barracks. I had seen him last in that hotel corridor in Belgrade in December, groggy with fatigue after a fruitless meeting with Milosevic, wondering aloud why the West was still, at the end of the twentieth century, liquidating the Ottoman empire. Few American officials know the south Balkans better. He had taken his first grades at the international school in Belgrade in the Fifties, when his father was political counselor at the American embassy. My father was a diplomat in Belgrade and I attended the same school. We reminisced for a minute about the indomitable Serbian spinsters who had been our teachers. Asked what impact a childhood in Belgrade had made on him, he said, 'it kept me from being anti-Serb.'

As a diplomat he had served throughout the whole inflamed region. In Albania, he had tried to help the democratically-elected President, Sali Berisha, pull the country out of chaos, only to watch it slide towards complete disintegration in 1997, when the Army's armories were looted and most of the country outside Tirana fell to family clans and their gunmen. He had been a key member of Richard Holbrooke's negotiating team at Dayton in 1995, which brought peace but also ethnic partition to Bosnia. Early in 1998, he had warned Washington that Kosovo was set to blow up. And during that autumn he shuttled between Pristina and Belgrade, trying to get both sides to negotiate; it was Hill who led the diplomacy at Rambouillet in February that persuaded the Albanians to put independence on hold and to disarm the KLA, before Milosevic rejected the deal out of hand. Now American diplomacy lay in ruins and he found himself guarded by Marines and a security detail in jeans and T-shirts who glided about in the background, large-caliber revolvers tucked into their belts in the small of their backs.

Hill does not wake at nights, replaying the tape of those

fruitless eighteen months. He sees no reason to apologize for negotiating with an unindicted war criminal. Every alternative to war had to be exhausted. In Rambouillet, in February, the inducements to Milosevic were considerable. It was not a negotiation designed to fail. It was not an ultimatum dictated at the point of a gun. In return for allowing NATO troops on his soil and a measure of autonomy for Kosovo, Milosevic would retain sovereignty over the province and would see his mortal enemy, the KLA, disarmed. If he had signed, Hill says, the Serbian people were offered 'an open road to the West.'

So why did Milosevic turn down the deal? The ambassador watched the Marines shoulder their M-16s and clump out to resume guard duty behind the sand-bags around his office. 'The honest answer is that I still don't know.' Maybe the 'road to the West' held no attractions to Milosevic's increasingly anti-Western electorate; maybe any deal signed by the KLA, men he saw as terrorists, was bound to be anathema; most likely, he never negotiated seriously at all. At Rambouillet, he played for time while positioning his troops for what became known as Operation Horseshoe – a decisive semicircular sweep around Kosovo designed to achieve a solution of his 'Kosovo problem.' Instead of negotiating a settlement, Milosevic went for broke, hoping that NATO would bomb, the alliance would crack and he would be left in full possession of Kosovo, having restored it to Serb hands forever.

A witty Macedonian friend – Saso Ordanoski who edits the monthly *Forum* – had warned me that the Balkans were not a Newtonian universe. Balkan physics was chaotically un-predictable. The war was the result of a double miscalculation. In his cynicism, Milosevic gambled that NATO would never go to war for its values. In our innocence, we gambled that he would never risk destruction for his.

Hill had said that Milosevic was a tactician not a strategist, capable of thinking only one move ahead on the chessboard. What diplomats failed to see – and so in truth did most writers and journalists – was that he was tenaciously consistent. From late 1990 the break-up of the former Yugoslavia became inevitable. Faced with the demand for independence and self-determination by its constituent republics, Milosevic followed one simple principle. Where there was no substantial Serb minority, as in Slovenia or Macedonia, he let them go. Where there was a Serb minority substantial enough for him to arm, he armed it and helped it to fight. The aim was to create defended Serbian enclaves throughout former Yugoslavia which one day would coalesce into a Greater Serbia under his leadership. The deaths of 250,000 people and the creation of more than a million refugees flow from his unwavering application of this principle. Rather than allow the peaceful self-determination of other ethnic groups, he armed the Serbs who were fighting for theirs. Rather than negotiate minority rights guarantees for Serbs in the successor states, he tried to destroy these states. And the West, lacking any equally consistent strategy for the dismemberment of Tito's state, let Milosevic have his way until they stopped him at Dayton. Dayton brought peace to Bosnia but it perpetuated an American illusion about Milosevic. They watched with astonishment as he traded away Sarajevo to the Muslims, betraying his Bosnian Serb clients. This led them to suppose that while he was an odious liar ('Believe me, I felt like washing my hands every time I came out of a meeting with the man,' says Dayton's chief architect Richard Holbrooke now) he was someone they could do business with. Success at Dayton led Americans to believe that they had the measure of the man. In reality, it was he who had the measure of them.

Milosevic managed to keep Kosovo out of the Dayton settlement – he refused to meet with an Albanian-American delegation who were pleading that Kosovo should be granted autonomy and that international observers should be dispatched to the province. He emerged from Dayton with his essential interests intact, and in the years that followed – when NATO troops failed to arrest the Bosnian war criminals, Mladic and Karadzic, responsible for the bombing of Sarajevo and the massacre at Srebrenica – he drew the conclusion that the West would talk about human rights and war crimes and do nothing.

Western observers and policy-makers observed the cynicism with which Milosevic betrayed fellow Serbs in Bosnia and assumed he would do the same in Kosovo. They noticed the dwindling Serb population in the province, down below ten per cent. They were taken in by all the Belgrade wits who used to joke in the 1980s that Serbs would do anything for Kosovo – except live there. They allowed themselves to believe a cheerfully cynical scenario: that we would pretend to bomb Milosevic, and he would pretend to resist and then a deal would be done, dropping a province he could no longer control into the lap of the international community. Certainly, this scenario helps to explain the homeopathic dose of bombing in the first phase of the campaign: the bombs were messages in a diplomatic game that the West supposed was still in progress. In reality, diplomacy was over: Milosevic had reached what Holbrooke called 'his red line.'

Milosevic could abandon the Serbs outside Serbia. But Kosovo was home ground: the location of the 'holy places,' the most ancient monasteries and churches of the Serbian

Orthodox faith, the site of that infamous defeat by the Turks in 1389, and above all a place where Serbs felt they were losing their homeland to the inexorable demographic increase of a population increasingly set on separation and independence. Milosevic had built his political career in Serbia on an intransigent defense of the Serbian minority in the province. To lose Kosovo, therefore, would be to lose all remaining legitimacy with his core support. In deciding to go to war he knew exactly where his ultimate interests lay, unlike Western leaders who believed, until far too late, that interests could be dissociated from values.

Once the bombing began, the objective shifted from getting Milosevic back to the negotiating table to 'prying his hands from the levers of power,' as one NATO general put it. But this was to misunderstand the nature of his regime. Just as he had pioneered ethnic cleansing and the use of refugees as a weapon of war, he had also pioneered the new style of post Cold War authoritarian populism. He was neither a Pinochet, dependent on the tanks, nor a Ceaucescu, dependent on the security police. His government was in fact a coalition of factions that loathed each other, but all of them duly elected by the people.

It was held to be an irony that bombing increased his popular support. In fact, he had always enjoyed a genuine popular base. As long as the bombing rallied his people around him, he could afford to lose military assets and the scenario of a military coup remained unlikely. He simply did not depend on the generals for his power. He was more vulnerable to a split within his coalition and to street demonstrations. Even these he was likely to face down, for there was an essential feature of Milosevic's character that rendered him especially resistant to both democratic and military pressure. This feature was more than ruthlessness or lack of scruple. No one in the West quite understood what Baton Haxhiu, the editor of Pristina's main Albanian newspaper, *Koha Ditore*, now in exile in Macedonia called Milosevic's 'incredible lightness of being,' his blithe indifference to all other human beings except himself, his wife and his immediate family. This indifference left him impervious to the sort of military pressure NATO could afford to bring to bear. NATO now awaited the capitulation of a man whose indifference to his own people's discomfort was a matter of record, and who might survive even if he did capitulate.

Nor did the West appreciate that Milosevic could afford to lose military assets because he was not fighting with conventional military means. Instead of fighting NATO in the air, he fought NATO on the air-waves. By allowing CNN and the BBC to continue broadcasting from inside Serbia, he hoped to destabilize and unsettle Western opinion with nightly stories of civilians carbonized in bombed trains and media workers incinerated by strikes on television stations. Propaganda has been central to war since the dawn of democracy, but it took an authoritarian populist from the Balkans to understand the awesome potential for influencing the opinion-base of an enemy, by manipulating modern real-time news to his own advantage. He gambled his regime on the tenderness of Western hearts, on the assumption that the Western public would not allow an air campaign to become murderous.

Now Pristina, Kosovo's capital, had been bombed. Its post office had been flattened and the phone-lines in the province were mostly dead. The oil depots and the Pristina corps barracks have been leveled.

Somewhere in those ruins or in a village outside were the

Albanian Kosovar negotiators who had signed the deal at Rambouillet which, had Milosevic also signed it, might have averted the war. They were one of the most unusual delegations in the history of diplomacy – a motley collection of guerilla commanders, newspaper editors and Westernized intellectuals, carpentered together by the Americans for the occasion and so unfamiliar with each other that most had never met until the moment they boarded the French military transport plane, taking them from Pristina to Rambouillet. One of them – Veton Surroi – had been crucial to getting the Albanian side to defer independence and agree to disarm the KLA. 'On fourth down, long yardage, with the seconds ticking away,' as Hill put it, Surroi had placed his prestige on the line to cajole the KLA leadership to sign. I had last seen Surroi, the dark-browed, elegantly dressed son of a former Yugoslav diplomat, at Pristina Airport in December telling Holbrooke what a coward Ibrahim Rugova was. Since then, Rugova had been forced to make a humiliating appearance side by side with Milosevic on Serbian television.

With Rugova discredited, Veton Surroi epitomized the new generation of Kosovar leaders who were gaining control of the Albanian movement. Where was he? All that Hill knew was that he and his mother were still alive, low on food, hiding in a basement in Pristina, whereabouts unknown. A man who only weeks ago had been savoring the cheese course at a French château in company with Secretary of State Albright and the Foreign Ministers of France and Britain was now huddling in the dark somewhere in Pristina, in fear of his life.

There were sixteen members of the Kosovo delegation at Rambouillet. Hashim Thaci, leader of the KLA, had escaped to Albania and then re-entered Kosovo with what remained of his guerilla units. Others were sheltering under the protection of KLA units on the run from the Serb sweep. Still others had struggled across the border into Macedonia. Hill thought I might be able to find one of them, Blerim Shala, an editor and political activist, whom I had last seen briefing Holbrooke at the now trashed and burned United States Information Service office in Pristina.

The search for Shala led me away from Skopje, through steep mountain roads, down to Debar, a rain-soaked town on the Albanian border, to a pizza parlor overlooking a sodden square. The barman served up freshly roasted hazel-nuts on a white paper plate which I nibbled as I waited for Shala, watching Albanian women in kerchiefs and long flowing trousers hopping across the puddles on their husbands' arms, while younger women, in jeans and T-shirts, emancipated from Muslim habits, smoked and joked with men taking shelter from the rain under the awning of the town's only functioning coffee bar.

Suddenly, Shala appeared – a slim, worn man in his thirties, several days of stubble on his angular face, wearing a wet jacket and jeans, in company with his silent brother-in-law. His change of fortune seemed to amaze rather than embitter him. 'Imagine,' he said, 'that a month ago I was shaking the hand of Mr William Cohen, the Secretary of Defense of the United States. And now? When I walk through the streets of this town at night, the Macedonian police stop me and threaten me with deportation,' until, he added, he informed them that the Macedonian government had given him resident status in their country.

The story he told – in quiet, nearly accentless English – was dramatic. After Rambouillet, the delegation had flown back to

Pristina in a French military aircraft, knowing that Milosevic
had turned down the deal, that air-strikes were imminent, and
that reprisals against them were inevitable. But the scope and
ferocity of these reprisals caught them by surprise. First the
paramilitaries killed the human rights lawyer Bajram Kelmendi
who had been collecting a dossier on Milosevic for a possible
indictment by The Hague tribunal for war crimes. After
Kelmendi's killing, Shala and the other members of the
delegation went into hiding, letting their beards grow, wearing
masks, keeping to the basement, watching the paramilitary
squads through the cellar windows as they cleared the Albanian
districts, block by block, house by house, apartment by
apartment. After four nights, Shala made a run for it with his
mother and brother and two children in a battered white Yugo.
Failing to make it to KLA-controlled areas, and seeing that
Pristina was ringed by roadblocks, they turned back and joined
a long line of cars making for the Macedonian border. Like
thousands of others, he spent two nights sleeping in the car,
before abandoning it and walking to the Serbian border post.
The Serb frontier guards knew immediately that he was a
member of the Rambouillet delegation. For two hours he
waited at the border while Belgrade made up its mind. Then
they waved him through. Repression, in other words, was fine-
tuned: the regime could decide, individual by individual, who
to let through, who to keep as a hostage. 'I'm not alive because
they missed me,' Shala said simply. 'I'm alive because they had
orders.' If his friend Surroi was still alive in Kosovo, Shala
believed, it was because Milosevic had decided it was to his
advantage. 'You can't hide from Serb security in Pristina,' Shala
said. Surroi's sister, in safety in Macedonia, disagreed. 'If they
find him, they kill him,' she said.

As Shala looked back at Rambouillet, it seemed to belong to another world. In the surreal gentility of the French château, the delegations never actually met. The Serb delegation was one floor below the Albanians, and they could hear the Serbs singing patriotic songs and carousing into the early hours. 'They simply did not negotiate at all.' What negotiation there was took place between the Americans and the Albanians, as Hill and Albright forced the Kosovars to defer independence and to disarm their guerillas. For Richard Holbrooke, now side-lined from the diplomacy by Albright, Rambouillet seemed like a chaotic waste of time: negotiating with one side, but not the other. But State Department spokesman James Rubin insists that the real point of Rambouillet was to persuade the Europeans, especially the Italians who tended to think of the Albanians as terrorists and drug traffickers, that they were actually 'the good guys.' Rambouillet was necessary, in other words, to get the Europeans to 'stop blaming the victims' and to build the resolve at NATO to use force.

Making concessions in order to make themselves salable to world opinion was a bitter pill, Shala confessed. And the delays that the KLA insisted upon to consult their field commanders gave Milosevic time to deploy his troops for the eviction of the Albanian population. The Serb leader had boasted to everyone who saw him in those final months – Wesley Clark and Holbrooke included – that all he needed was a few weeks to finish off 'the terrorists.' His intentions were never hidden, though the scale of the operation exceeded the most pessimistic predictions of NATO intelligence.

As they settled into exile, whiling away the hours in the Albanian male-only cafés of Macedonia, intellectuals like Shala and the newspaper editor Baton Haxhiu had time to rue their own miscalculations. These were men who believed in late 1997 that a strategy of non-violence in Kosovo was getting nowhere: Serb repression was getting worse; Western governments were looking the other way. Haxhiu had secret conversations in late 1997 with top-ranking Serb security personnel who warned him that if the Kosovars persisted with their demands for independence, they would 'burn every one of your villages to the ground.'

When this was reported to the Americans, they did not react. American policy-makers projected a tender conscience about human rights violations, but as long as the Kosovo problem seemed a human rights problem alone, they did nothing. They actually accepted, at least tacitly, Milosevic's argument that he was facing a secessionist movement using terror tactics, and that his reprisals, while severe, were within a state's legitimate right of self-defence. At the same time, the Americans treated Milosevic with respect, as a guarantor of the Dayton peace settlement in Bosnia. American indifference to Serb repression of the Kosovars, Haxhiu said, was one reason why his generation decided to support the KLA. Indeed, they took a lesson from the Bosnian Serbs. They had used violence to secure a state – Republika Srpska – for themselves and Dayton had ratified their territorial conquests. The Kosovars decided to copy their enemy – in the expectation that the international community would also ratify what they took by force. From the middle of 1997, young guerilla commanders based in Albania, who purchased arms aboard in Europe, began striking at post offices, barracks and police stations inside Kosovo. In a scant few months, they did more to put the Serbs on the defensive than a decade of non-violent protest, and by the summer of 1998, Western governments were at last awaking to the fact that Kosovo was no longer a human rights issue: there was a full-scale civil war in the province, threatening to spread to other states in the region.

But the KLA drastically over-reached themselves and their tactical choices, Haxhiu believed, were catastrophic. Hit and run attacks on Serb military and police targets exposed civilians to reprisals. Then they tried to liberate villages and towns, which they had neither the arms nor the men to hold. As soon as they were driven out, the Serbs massacred or evicted the population. It is more than possible, of course, that KLA tactics were not a miscalculation, but a deliberate strategy, designed to incite the Serbs to commit massacres that would eventually force NATO to intervene. Besides exposing their own civilian support to vicious reprisals, the KLA made drastic political and diplomatic miscalculations. They demanded full independence for Kosovo as a step towards a Greater Albania. Neither the Europeans nor the Americans had any appetite for altering existing frontiers and the prospect of an independent Kosovo terrified neighboring countries – Macedonia, Greece and Montenegro – with substantial ethnic Albanian minorities. The extremists in the KLA believed they could change American minds by making Kosovo ungovernable. Instead they had unleashed *Götterdammerung*, Milosevic's expulsion of their entire nation. Now, in the cafés of Macedonia, there was plenty of time for Baton Haxhiu and Blerim Shala to repent at leisure for their support of the KLA, to realize that they did not want the KLA to emerge as the political and military beneficiary of a NATO victory. Chris Hill had said that the KLA were never likely to win 'the Thomas Jefferson award for citizenship.' They wanted the power that comes at the point of a gun, and when they got it, they would turn it on any Serbs who remained, and on any democratic Kosovars who opposed them. Baton Haxhiu sometimes asks himself what he fought for: 'We do not need political commissars in Kosovo.'

Now that the bombs were falling, and the West had entered the dark tunnel of a war it saw no clear way of ending quickly, it was easy to conclude that all the mistakes were American ones. But if America misjudged Milosevic, he also fatally misjudged America. A case in point was Racak. This small village, near Pristina, figures in everyone's recollections as one of the precipitating causes of the war. On the evening of 15 January, William Walker, the head of the Kosovo Verification Mission, received a call from his British deputy, General John Drewenkiewicz, that something unusual had occurred at Racak. Walker set out next morning in a small convoy of orange armored Chevrolet Suburbans. They reached the village at about 10:30 on a bitterly cold Saturday morning. Distraught women pointed Walker and his party to a ravine at the back of the village, and there Walker came upon a body under a blanket. When he pulled back the blanket, he saw that the body was headless. Up the slippery, ice-filled ravine he climbed, past body after body, farm workers in muddy boots and overalls, their clothing wet with urine and blood and old men with grizzled beards, face down in the snow. At the top of the ravine, a pile of bodies. The observers counted forty-five in all.

Survivors told how paramilitaries had invaded the village, searching for a KLA unit, separated the men, marched them into the ravine and standing above them on the sides, fired down, killing them where they knelt. Having seen for himself, Walker did not clear his next move with Washington. At a press conference immediately afterwards, he called the Racak massacre a crime against humanity and left no one in any doubt who was responsible. Other American officials, like Chris Hill, were appalled, because the denunciation appeared to bring the Verification Mission squarely down on the side of the KLA at a time when human rights violations were occurring on both sides. Within forty-eight hours Milosevic had declared him persona non grata, and while Walker defied his expulsion order and stayed on, the monitoring mission was effectively over: its cars stoned, Walker himself threatened, his verification monitors in danger.

Milosevic had miscalculated: he drove the monitors out, but Racak proved critical in the Administration's attempts to mobilize the European members of NATO to take military action. Until then, the Serbs had calibrated their repression in Kosovo to a level they believed NATO would have to accept. NATO's Secretary General, Javier Solana, had been circulating a grim little joke reportedly made by a Serb diplomat: 'A village a day keeps NATO away.' Racak was supposed to be just another village massacre: thanks to Walker and the monitors, it proved to be one too many. Without Racak, air-strikes would never have happened. With Walker's reaction to Racak, the Americans began tipping their hand in favor of the KLA. This led Milosevic to break off with the Americans. When Holbrooke went to see Milosevic in March, the Serb leader refused to negotiate and instead raged that the Americans were now siding openly with the 'terrorists.' Holbrooke returned to Washington certain that the war was inevitable.

Milosevic now made a deeper miscalculation, assuming that when it came to the use of force, the Clinton Administration and its European allies would prove as vacillating in Kosovo as they had been in Bosnia. In Bosnia, an inexperienced

Administration first scuppered a European peace initiative – the Vance-Owen peace plan – in February 1993; then proposed arming the Muslims and striking the Serbs from the air, only to lack the resolve to push this through over European hesitation; and then stood back and watched the United Nations peace-keeping effort fall apart, culminating in the Srebrenica massacre of July 1995. Four years later, Milosevic concluded that this catastrophic failure of will would repeat itself in Kosovo.

Since the Bosnia debacle, American resolve had stiffened. There was a new Secretary of State, Madeleine Albright, the daughter of a Czech diplomat forced into exile after Munich, who was especially sensitive to the appearance of appeasement. (Her spokesman, James Rubin, recalls the diplomatic conference in London on January 29, 1999, convened to prepare the final negotiating position with the Serbs, at which he proposed some bland face-saving formula for the final communiqué only to find himself dressed down in public by his Secretary of State: 'This is London, remember,' she boomed, 'not Munich.') Kosovo could not be this Administration's Munich.

And although Holbrooke had warned him explicitly that the NATO bombing campaign would be 'swift and sustained,' Milosevic ignored evidence that the Administration's pro-pensity to bomb had increased sharply from its days of fumbling indecision over Bosnia. The accuracy of new airborne weapons systems lowered – or appeared to lower – the political costs of using them. Clinton went to war, believing that new technology would bring speedy, risk-free victory. At the beginning of his Presidency, Tomahawk missiles could take out discrete buildings. By April 1999, the missiles were sufficiently precise to strike the Serbian leader's very bedroom. Such weaponry appeared to offer America guilt-free war. That was the theory: in practice, there are never any silver bullets. Targets were missed and innocent civilians were killed, and even when they hit the targets, the weapons didn't finish the job. With the candour which comes when military leaders believe they must distance themselves from flawed political instructions, generals in charge of the campaign were soon making it explicit that the air campaign also could not work. At the end of April, General Wesley Clark, the Supreme Allied Commander, was commendably frank: after six weeks of bombing, there were more Serb forces inside Kosovo than when the bombing began. The air campaign alone could neither halt ethnic cleansing nor avoid mounting civilian casualties.

High tech warfare is governed by two constraints – avoiding civilian casualties and avoiding risks to pilots – that are in direct contradiction. To target effectively you have to fly low. If you fly low, you lose pilots. Fly high and you get civilians. Low-flying Apache helicopters could both target ethnic cleansers and avoid civilian casualties, but by week six the alliance had not even approved their deployment in Kosovo, believing that risks to crews from ground fire were still too high. As the campaign went into its second month, the alliance's moral preferences were clear: preserving the lives of their all-volunteer service professionals was a higher priority than saving innocent foreign civilians. This was the moral calculus of war throughout the ages, but in a television age, it has a political cost: would the public at home continue to stand rising civilian casualties if the bombing was not having any discernible military effect?

To Britain's Tony Blair, the alliance leader most obviously animated by cold fury and relentless conviction, it seemed apparent that military success required taking some real risks.

After months in which the American Administration presented itself as driving the reluctant Europeans, suddenly the Europeans, led by the British, appeared to be pushing for ground troops. But the President hesitated, hoping against mounting evidence that the bombing would be sufficient.

Having ruled out a forced entry into Kosovo, on the grounds that casualties would be too high, the President was now totally dependent on precision lethality from high altitudes. The question was: who would crack first, the Serbian regime or a Western public, disgusted by carnage apparently disconnected from any believable winning strategy?

Either the bombing would work and Serbia would capitulate, or a stalemate would lead to a diplomatic solution. In the first outcome, Serbia would be bombed into surrendering and NATO would enter Kosovo unopposed. The refugees would return and the province would be made a NATO protectorate indefinitely. In the second scenario, stalemate, the Russians would intervene to dictate a settlement. The Serbs would continue to hold sovereignty over Kosovo and a UN force with a Russian contingent would go in to supervise a truce. The Russians, however, were still not ready to assume that role. As one Russian official told a senior Western diplomat, 'we have many Kosovos of our own.' They were alarmed by the prospect of a victorious and expanded NATO, right up against their Western frontier, now tasking itself with interference in their internal conflicts. These were among the fears that the American Administration had to soothe. Yet senior Western officials, who had dealt with President Yeltsin and his envoy Victor Chernomyrdin, maintained that eventually the Russians would co-operate. The Russians supported the Serbs in public, but in private their arguments with Milosevic's brother, the

Yugoslav ambassador to Moscow, were loud enough, according to Strobe Talbott, 'for us to hear down the street.' In weeks, rather than months, Western officials hoped, the Russians would force their Serbian clients to sign a surrender.

But what if neither bombing nor diplomacy worked? What if Milosevic refused to capitulate? NATO might declare the aggressor punished, announce victory and return its bombers to base. But a deported Albanian nation, in exile in the camps, could not be disguised. Even Henry Kissinger, long an opponent of Albright's moralizing interventionism, had publicly declared, once the bombing began, that NATO could not be allowed to fail. If it did, the entire strategic architecture, linking American and European interests since World War II, would be in ruins.

The remaining option was the use of ground troops. While no one at NATO would say so explicitly, the existing air campaign was clearly designed to prepare the entry for NATO ground troops, by pounding Serb forces, destroying tanks and artillery, flattening munitions dumps and oil supplies. If Milosevic managed to withstand these blows, no one was prepared to say what numbers of troops would be required to suppress remaining Serb resistance. An American military suspicious of its Commander-in-Chief's ultimate resolve might well insist on full enforcement of the Colin Powell doctrine: overwhelming superiority, colossal logistical back-up, massive, persistent and all-encompassing operations. But this would take time, and would probably defer a ground assault until after the autumn rains and winter snows. Meanwhile, the Albanian nation in exile under canvas would freeze to death.

This left a more risky strategy that relied not on over-whelming force, but on speed and high-tempo maneuver: parachute regiments could be lifted over the mountains and dropped along key supply roads; Apache helicopter teams could target Serb forces on the ground, and Marine troops, dispatched from NATO warships in the Adriatic, could establish entry corridors down which would begin to flow tanks, artillery and more ground troops. They would, however, face an experienced army with two important assets: superior knowledge of the terrain and one of Europe's strongest traditions of partisan guerilla war. These would make them difficult to beat. The Serbs would want to fight asymmetrically, avoiding full battle, breaking into small units, seeking not to win, but to down sufficient helicopters and kill enough troops to break NATO's resolve. These prospects were sobering for even the most convinced interventionist. NATO defeat – and anything less than Milosevic's capitulation and the full return of the refugees would be a defeat – would leave the two global civilizations, Europe and America, without a credible defense alliance.

America had gone to war to save the Kosovars; now it was waking to the reality that it had to build a durable peace for a whole region. The hard truth, as some American diplomats in the region admitted, was that America never had a coherent Balkans policy. It reacted to Milosevic; it never succeeded in anticipating his game. For a decade, America's policies had been driven by massacre, crisis and catastrophe. Now it had to devise a policy response equal to the size of the chaos Milosevic had unleashed. But in an administration, where 'the urgent,' in one American diplomat's words, is 'always crowding out the important,' creating a new security architecture for the whole region was a daunting task. A ravaged, burned and bombed Kosovo would have to be rebuilt from scratch. And what was at stake was suddenly much larger than Kosovo. Macedonia, with its agonizingly poised ethnic mix and shaky coalition government, would have to be stabilized with a NATO security guarantee. Montenegro, still a republic unwillingly yoked to Serbia inside the Federal Republic of Yugoslavia, needed protection. A protectorate for Kosovo logically implied a protectorate for Montenegro too. Albania, reeling under the impact of the refugee crisis, was a country without a state, and had to be stabilized if there was ever to be peace in the region. Bulgaria and Romania, Serbia's neighbors to the east, needed protection from the Russians. America – the reluctant empire – was suddenly being asked, by every small country in the region, to be the guarantor of their peace and security. Of course the Europeans could provide money, expertise and humanitarian help. But the leadership had to come from a nation uninterested in the Balkans and unconvinced of the strategic importance of the region. Long-term commitments like rebuilding the Balkans peace are never easy for a liberal democracy and may be especially difficult for this one, since the Administration is in its last years. In the past, a change in Administration has been fatal in the Balkans: Bosnia nearly perished in late 1992 and early 1993 as Bush handed over to Clinton. If the Democrats lose in November 2000, the Administration that finally found the nerve to intervene in Kosovo might have to hand over to a team as untried as Clinton's was in January 1993.

In the short time available, the challenge was daunting: to forge policies for southern and eastern Europe as large and generous as those conceived by Marshall, Truman and Acheson for central and northern Europe in the 1940s. The President and the British Prime Minister seemed to grasp these larger implications. At least the words were there, in the promise of a stability pact for southern Europe, to include Serbia if its leadership were to change. Whether the commitment is there only time will tell.

Back in Stankovec 2, the refugees gathered in the darkness of their tents to make agonizing choices of their own. Promises had been made to them: Strobe Talbott in Macedonia had said they would be going home. William Walker had toured a camp and made the same pledge. But when? Families gathered in conclaves to decide whether to accept the offer of a place in a camp in Trier, Germany, or to stay in the camp to be ready to follow the troops back up the road to Pristina. I listened as families struggled to make sense in private personal ways of the geo-political struggle unleashed over their heads. With children dozing in their laps, parents sat cross-legged on the tent floor, leaning together, heads touching, trying to make choices which might change their and their children's lives forever.

They knew that if they stayed they risked becoming trapped like so many Bosnian refugees, some of them still in camps in Macedonia five years after the fighting stopped; if they left, they might never see Kosovo again. I listened, and when asked for advice, I tried not to deceive them. The Administration was hesitating; the earliest troops could be ready for ground operations was late summer; and if they stayed in the camps, they risked being trapped by the winter snows. Most reluctantly boarded the buses for the airport to board planes for Germany. They were weeping. The camps were no place for children. The families had no time to wait for men in Washington and Brussels to steel themselves for the next level of moral risk.

May, 1999

THE WAR OF WORDS: A
DIALOGUE ON INTERVENTION

Robert Skidelsky and Michael Ignatieff
(Photo courtesy of *Prospect*.)

The War of Words: A
Dialogue on Intervention

In late April, I came back from the refugee camps in Macedonia, convinced that intervention had been necessary, as well as overdue. But I returned to a country – Britain – which was deeply divided by both the morality and the tactics of the war. NATO bombs had already struck the Belgrade television station and the refugees in a convoy on the Djakovica road. These catastrophes brought home the difficulty of justifying the war in terms of human rights. For how could such arguments justify killing the people you were supposed to protect?

The ensuing debate in Britain illustrated a point that Isaiah Berlin, the liberal philosopher, had been at pains to emphasize: that intense disagreement often occurs between people sharing the same premises. People equally committed to human rights disagreed fundamentally on the morality of war. Moreover, as

Berlin also argued, such disagreements were often irreconcilable. The debate divided friends as much as it reinforced the divide between enemies. Finally, as Berlin also insisted, choosing was hard: it was not just a simple matter of plumping for good against evil, but sustaining a commitment to good ends even when the means adopted were questionable.[1]

Kosovo made it obvious that wars waged in the name of values invariably turn out to be more controversial than wars waged for interests. Maintaining popular support for humanitarian intervention required unrelenting media management by NATO and the political leadership of the alliance countries, and even when spun round the clock by generals, spokesmen and leaders, the public became more, rather than less skeptical towards arguments for the war as it progressed.

The dominant question in the public debate among the NATO countries was whether they had the right to intervene militarily in the affairs of a sovereign state. In an important speech in Chicago on April 22, Prime Minister Blair argued that the NATO campaign on behalf of the Kosovars had shifted the balance between human rights and state sovereignty.[2] The presumption enshrined in the UN Charter that states should not resort to war except in self-defense and that they should be immune from intervention by other sovereign states had now to be revised. Acts of genocide, he said, could never remain a purely internal matter. Likewise, oppression which led to massive flows of refugees could not be allowed to stand. If such conditions mandated intervention in principle, he went on, we also had to ask practical questions before we sent the troops in. First, are we sure of our case? Second, have we exhausted all diplomatic options? Third, are there military operations 'we can sensibly and prudently undertake'? Fourth, are we prepared for the long-term? And finally, do we have national interests involved? If we could answer these questions in the affirmative, we should intervene. The Prime Minister believed the Kosovo intervention cleared these hurdles.

In Britain, the Prime Minister's speech triggered a substantial debate on the morality of the NATO intervention. *Prospect* magazine, a liberal monthly, invited me and the independent member of the House of Lords, Robert Skidelsky, to take part in a debate on the right of intervention. Robert Skidelsky is a distinguished biographer of John Maynard Keynes, and a liberal political economist and philosopher with centrist and pragmatic views similar to my own.[3] Nevertheless, we disagreed completely, as the ensuing exchange of letters should indicate. It was, by the way, a virtual exchange: we never met face to face, since Skidelsky was traveling in Australia at the time, and the letters are in fact e-mails.

May 3, 1999
Dear Michael,

I have been instinctively against NATO's bombing of Serbia from the day it started on 24th March. I was – I dare say like you and many others – incredulous that NATO seemed to have no military strategy except to bomb Serbia to smithereens. I could not believe that bombing a defenceless country was the right way to wage 'holy war.' But above all I was alarmed by the thought that a new doctrine of international relations was being forged which would make the world a much more dangerous place.

That is what I want to discuss. Given that NATO's values are superior to Milosevic's values, is it right or prudent to try to force our values on him? Until recently, most of us have signed up to quite a different doctrine of international relations. The UN was founded on the principle of national sovereignty. States could and should be sanctioned for acts of aggression against other states, but within their borders they were free (with one large caveat) to do what they liked. You might say that this was a pretty minimal basis for world order. But the UN was founded on prudential, not ethical rules, and it was a great advance to get states to sign up to them.

Now to the caveat. Chapter Seven of the UN Charter says that states can be sanctioned for actions which are a 'threat to peace.' This allows the UN to take into account the spillover effects of domestic policies – if, for example, they produce floods of refugees or destabilize other states. But human rights abuse per se is not a ground for intervention (Pinochet's Chile was never sanctioned). This is for the good reason that there is no international agreement on the standards to be upheld and the means to uphold them.

The old imperialism had its own way of overcoming this problem. Advanced states conquered 'barbarous' ones and imposed 'civilized standards' on them. But as even Churchill conceded, this process had become 'contrary to the ethics of the twentieth century.' Not, apparently, to the ethics of Tony Blair. In his Chicago speech on 22 April he advanced what he called 'The Doctrine of International Community.' Globalization, he said, means 'We cannot turn our backs on the violation of human rights in other countries if we want to be secure.' This fact required an 'important qualification' to the principle of non-interference. The UN Charter should be amended to make this possible. And Blair was insistent that having made a commitment to intervene, 'we cannot simply walk away once the fight is over: better to stay with a moderate number of troops than return for repeat performances.'

Blair takes direct issue with the prudential tradition of diplomacy. 'Bismarck,' he remarked, 'famously said that the Balkans were not worth the bones of a single Pomeranian grenadier.' He added smugly: 'Bismarck was wrong.' Who would you have preferred to be in charge in 1914: Bismarck or Blair?

Blair wants international co-operation on the basis of agreed values and rules. But NATO did not agree on the values or rules with Russia, China or anyone else before it started bombing Serbia. Nor did it seek UN authorization. Thank goodness Russia is doing what it can to find a compromise, but its official line is that the bombing of Serbia was an 'act of aggression' which flouts the UN Charter and international law. Moreover, Foreign Minister Ivanov says NATO's attempt to 'tear Kosovo out of Yugoslavia' threatens Russia's own relations with its Islamic minorities. We stand at a fork in international affairs. Does the West have carte blanche to make its values prevail whenever it has the temporary power to do so? Or will it confine its ethical ambitions to limits acceptable to other great powers with different values and interests?

Let me end with four assertions and one question. First, there is no international consensus on the standards expected of states in dealing with their own subjects or on the sanctions appropriate to breaches of agreed standards. Second, NATO failed to seek UN authorization for its attack on Serbia because it knew it would not get it. Third, the by-passing of the UN by NATO sends a clear message to all countries that force, not law, governs international affairs. Fourth, if membership of the UN no longer protects states from invasion, all governments which can, will acquire weapons of mass destruction to deter or repel foreign invasion. Now the question: do you really think that the West has the guts to fight its way into other countries and occupy them for indefinite periods of time?

Yours,

Robert Skidelsky.

May 4, 1999

Dear Robert

I couldn't disagree with you more, but we need to clear away the areas of common ground in order to figure out exactly where our disagreement lies. I agree with you that there should be a general presumption in favor of state sovereignty in international affairs. Such a presumption provides alibis for dictators, but it also protects weak but democratic states from more powerful neighbors. Where states are democratic, their sovereignty is also an expression of their people's right to self-determination. So there are reasons of principle not to interfere in states whose internal affairs we find disagreeable. I also accept that human rights abuses, by themselves, do not legitimize military intervention. Other kinds of 'soft' intervention – formal protests, assistance to persecuted groups, boycotts and sanctions – are preferable. Military intervention should always be an instrument of absolute last resort. So the question is to define when human rights abuses in another country justify that last resort. I believe that armed intervention can only be justified in two instances: first, when human rights abuses rise to the level of a systematic attempt to expel or exterminate large numbers of people who have no means of defending themselves; second, where these abuses threaten the peace and security of neighboring states.

Two further conditions should be added: first, all diplomatic alternatives must have been exhausted; second, force can only be justified when it stands a real chance of working. Force can't be justified simply to punish, avenge or signify moral outrage. It must be a credible way to stop abuses and restore peace.

Before we consider whether the Kosovo situation meets these criteria, we must clear away another matter. You maintain that there is 'no international consensus on the standards expected of states in dealing with their own subjects.' This is not the case. Since Nuremberg, since the Universal Declaration of Human Rights, there has been a set of international norms on the internal conduct of states which those who sign these conventions – and Yugoslavia is a signatory – are supposed to abide by. So the problem about intervention does not lie, as you suppose, in the relativity of international norms. Serbia's violation of these norms in Kosovo is not a matter of serious dispute. These norms exist; the problem is whether an international right of intervention should trump state sovereignty in the case of the Serb abuses in Kosovo.

In my view Kosovo does meet the strict criteria for a justified intervention. A defenceless people have been driven from their homes and their arrival in Albania and Macedonia is destabilizing a strategically important region. Your position – to stay out and do nothing – is sustainable only on the assumption that Milosevic is telling the truth, and that the deportees were driven out by NATO bombing. Having just spent a week in the camps in Macedonia, talking to families evicted from Pristina, I am in no doubt that the ethnic cleansing was systematically planned before the NATO bombing. Western intelligence confirms that Operation Horseshoe was already under way before the first NATO air-strikes.

You make a crucial concession: that Chapter Seven of the UN Charter mandates interventions in cases where domestic policies 'produce floods of refugees or destabilize other states'. This is precisely the case in Kosovo. Serbian policy has never been a strictly internal matter: in Kosovo, Milosevic decided to solve an 'internal' human rights problem by exporting an entire nation to his impoverished neighbors. His actions have bequeathed chaos to a whole region and guaranteed that there will be armed conflict until the Kosovars can rule themselves free of Serb repression.

In understanding why we have a right to intervene militarily, we also need to understand Milosevic's consistent attempt to deny the right of self-determination to anyone except his own Serbian people. He chose war, rather than peace, in 1991, when Slovenia and Croatia exercised their rights of self-determination. In 1992, he armed an insurrection against a UN recognized state, Bosnia. It is difficult to respect the territorial integrity and sovereignty of a state which has shown such disregard for the integrity and sovereignty of its neighbors. His regime has been a clear and present danger to the stability of an entire region of Europe for nine years.

The second area of disagreement between us is whether military intervention can be justified without explicit UN sanction and approval. In principle, member states should seek approval of the use of force from the Security Council. The veto system in the council can provide a useful break on imperialist misadventure. But the veto system has also prevented the UN from intervening when it should have done. Sticking only to the most recent and relevant instances, the UN Security Council's failure to prevent genocide in both Rwanda and Bosnia has made it essential that where a veto threatens to make the international community complicit in evil, coalitions of member states should be able to act on their own. I appreciate that this entails risks, but coalitions can exert restraints on their more excitable members. NATO is much condemned for waging war by committee, but it is precisely because nineteen member states must be persuaded before military action can be undertaken, that such action has not become indiscriminate or disproportionate.

You say, finally, that NATO action will send a message that force, rather than law, governs international affairs. There are occasions, on the contrary, when if force is not used there is no future for law. Failure to reverse the most meticulous deportation of a civilian population since the Second World War would have set a fatal precedent wherever authoritarian leaders believe that force should substitute for dialogue in their domestic affairs.

Yours,

Michael Ignatieff

May 6, 1999
Dear Michael,

You define several fruitful areas of disagreement between us. The first concerns the importance to be attached to the principle of non-interference in the domestic affairs of states. You admit that there is a 'general presumption' in favor of non-interference, but you qualify this so heavily as almost to turn it into its opposite. That is, you seem to believe that intervention is justified whenever human rights are violated, but must be proportional to the offence. Military force is reserved for two cases: genocide or mass expulsion; and when human rights abuses threaten the peace and security of neighboring states. Since, as Tony Blair admits, there are 'many regimes . . . engaged in barbarous acts,' the scope for intervention is in principle huge. Moreover, since NATO (or rather the US) has overwhelming air superiority almost everywhere, your prudential qualification, 'only when force has a real chance of working,' is less than it seems.

You also weaken the presumption of non-interference unduly by omitting the most compelling argument in its favor, namely that it offers the only secure basis for good (and peaceful) interstate relations in a world where values differ. This has been the conclusion of three centuries of European stagecraft, first enunciated at the Treaty of Westphalia. Perhaps you rate justice higher than peace. If so, this is a disagreement between us.

This brings me to your contention that all UN members accept the same norms of domestic behaviour. You cite Nuremberg verdicts and the Universal Declaration of Human Rights. I accept that Nuremberg gave legal force to two universally accepted norms: that genocide and the planning and waging of aggressive war are wicked and should always be prevented or punished. The fact that we have not acted on the first since the Second World War is a dreadful blot.

I doubt if there is genuine consensus on much else. You seem to believe that when states sign up to lists of rights they all think that they mean the same thing. This is a familiar Western (particularly American) delusion and I'm surprised you fall for it. I'm talking about substantive agreement, not legal decoration.

Even assuming more agreement than is the case, the practical problems nearly always arise when norms conflict. The classic case is when two ethnic or religious groups have claims on the same territory and cannot work out a *modus vivendi*. In such a case, separation (which always involves some ethnic cleansing) may be the best solution. Yet this was never on the table at Rambouillet, despite the fact that there have been many relatively successful postwar examples, such as the separation of Jews and Arabs in Palestine, or of Greeks and Turks in Cyprus. Our inability to accept that large parts of the world do not work according to Western rules has brought enormous troubles on us and those we succor.

You say that force should only be used when it is a 'credible way to stop abuses and restore peace.' But do you seriously believe that NATO bombing is a credible method of achieving these goals? There is nothing more immoral than making promises to endangered people and then leaving them to their fate.

Finally, you rather airily wave aside the objection that NATO is making war on a member of the UN without UN authorization. The veto is not an inconvenient obstacle to humanitarian designs. It is there to ensure international consensus for UN intervention. Such a consensus does not exist in the Security Council – most members of the UN are opposed to the NATO bombing.

This does not mean that 'stay out and do nothing' is the only option; nor do I believe Milosevic's propaganda. Had NATO accepted from 1998 that force was ruled out without clear evidence of genocide or mass expulsion, the diplomacy would have been different. A joint approach would have been hammered out between the US, the EU and Russia as the basis of any demands on Serbia. At this stage, NATO should not have been involved at all.

It was NATO's willingness to use force without achieving a Great Power consensus which is directly responsible for this tragic turn of events – from which we now rely on Russia to rescue us.

Yours,

Robert.

7 May, 1999
Dear Robert,

Our disagreement is wider than the issue of Kosovo. We have different views of the international system itself. This is a disagreement about facts as well as their implication. You are a Westphalian: for you the only relevant actors in the international system are states; their inviolability is all but absolute; and there are no agreed norms to regulate their conduct other than the obligation not to commit genocide or wage aggressive war. I am an internationalist: states have rights and immunities but so do individuals. When these rights are violated, individuals have recourse in law to human rights bodies in the UN system. When persecuted individuals or national groups have exhausted all remedies and stand defenceless before aggression in their home state, they have the right to appeal and to receive humanitarian and even military assistance. Contrary to what you say, I construe the grounds for military interventions narrowly: they should always be a last resort, when all peaceful means of assisting a vulnerable population had been exhausted.

We also disagree about the cross-cultural validity of human rights norms. Unlike you, I believe there is a widening range of internationally agreed norms for the conduct of both international and domestic policy. We are not living in the culturally relative moral world that you describe. All nations formally accept that torture, rape, massacre and forcible expulsion are violations of international humanitarian law. There is no substantive intercultural dispute as to whether such abuses have occurred in Kosovo or whether they violate international norms of conduct.

You dismiss this structure of international human rights law as nothing more than the homage which vice pays to virtue. I do not deny that states honor these obligations more in the breach than in the observance, but it seems incontrovertible that international rights norms do operate as a real constraint on the domestic behavior of a growing number of states. If the conduct of states were as you describe, Serbia's behavior in Kosovo would not be the exception it is. No other state in Europe commits such violations of internationally agreed norms.

You construe attempts by outsiders to monitor human rights in other states as a meddlesome post-imperial moralism, attempting to apply 'Western rules where these do not apply.' But the mandate to intervene comes not just from 'our' side but from 'theirs.' Our military intervention in the Balkans is not imposing moral standards on a people who do not accept their validity. On the contrary: Kosovar Albanians have been begging for our assistance in the face of more than twelve years of increasing Serbian repression.

As to the specifics of what you propose in relation to Kosovo. You suggest that the West should have negotiated with Milosevic on the basis of a joint approach hammered out between the US, EU and Russia. You seem to forget that this is exactly what happened: such an approach was agreed by the Contact Group, which included Russians. It respected the

territorial integrity of Yugoslavia, insisted that the KLA
insurgents be disarmed and provided for explicit guarantees of
Serb minority rights and protection of their holy places. Such a
deal offered a credible solution to the Kosovo crisis because it
respected the essential national interests of the Serbian people.
Milosevic turned it down.

You maintain that the tragedy has occurred because the
West resorted to force without first securing a Great Power
consensus. On the contrary, the tragedy occurred because
Milosevic thought that he could divide Russia and the West,
and get away with a final solution of the Kosovo problem.

Your suggestion that the ethnic groups be separated
logically implies partition – which in turn implies a substantial
erosion of the sovereignty of Yugoslavia. If this is your position,
it contradicts your support for non-interference. In any event,
partition is impractical, because both communities are
distributed throughout the province, as are their cultural and
religious sites. This leaves either complete independence for
Kosovo or a UN protectorate. If it is to be independence, the
Serbs have to understand that it is their conduct that has lost
them the territory.

As for the UN, the Secretary-General himself has said that
the resort to force can be justified in Kosovo, because there is a
threat to the peace and security of the region. You yourself
concede that the deportation of an entire nation constitutes
such a threat, yet you do not commit yourself to any practical
action which would restore these people to their homes. Your
objections are focused on the failure to secure UN approval.
The Western countries are not bypassing the UN: as the recent
G7 negotiating position makes clear, the Russians are now
prepared to approve a resolution in the Security Council

mandating a deployment with NATO troops at its core. This would return the whole operation under a UN umbrella where it belongs. The real obstacle to a settlement remains Milosevic himself. It is disingenuous to claim that only one side in this dispute has failed to abide by the UN Charter: the list of UN resolutions which Milosevic has ignored or violated is exceedingly long.

As for the bombing, I framed my conditions for the use of military force in the belief that force can only be justified if it achieves precise military objectives. If Milosevic agrees to negotiate a settlement which allows for the refugees to return under international protection, then the bombing should cease at once. If he refuses to negotiate, the bombing should continue until Serb forces are sufficiently weakened to permit a ground invasion of Kosovo, whose aim would be to occupy the province, disarm Serb forces, return the refugees, rebuild the province, place it under UN administration and then exit as soon as a permanent ceasefire could be negotiated with the Serbs. A bombing campaign which is not geared to this objective, and which simply continues to destroy the infrastructure of Serbia and kill civilians, would have nobody's support in the long term. The bombing must be directed at military targets with the aim of introducing ground troops as soon as possible.

Yours,
Michael

8 May, 1999
Dear Michael,

Evidently we disagree both about the nature of the international system and about the facts of the case. What you see as the actually existing international order, I see as a project to refashion it according to Western norms. I believe strongly in these norms. But the attempt to conduct international relations as though all these states accepted them can only serve to make the world more war-prone. This is why I am, as you say, a Westphalian. One must always remember, though, that the system of 'live and let live' did not exclude agreed action by the Great Powers if a domestic conflict threatened international peace.

This brings me to the facts. I am amazed that you continue to believe that Russia at any time supported the NATO solution. The bombing in particular has united all Russians, from liberals to communists, in opposition to NATO action. Yeltsin has ordered the development of new tactical nuclear missiles to counter a perceived increased threat from NATO. So much for Russia being 'on side.'

Historians will argue about when or whether Milosevic's savage reprisals against the KLA turned into a deliberate program of ethnic cleansing. What is undeniable is that the mass exodus from Yugoslavia started after the bombing started. I would have expected more scepticism from you about NATO's claims. My main point, though, is that the NATO action has made the world a more dangerous place.

Yours,

Robert

10 May, 1999
Dear Robert,

You can only maintain your position by misrepresenting the facts. Ethnic cleansing was under way in Kosovo ten months before the bombing began. The departure of the Kosovar Albanians was not an 'exodus,' but systematic deportation, using military units. You argue as if these facts were still in dispute: but the facts are plain. They constitute the worst political crime in Europe since 1945.

You cling to the fiction that diplomacy might have averted war, and argue that we didn't do enough to line up the Russians behind diplomatic pressure. What do you suppose was going on between May 1998 and March 1999? You forget that the Russians were at Rambouillet and that they did everything they could to get the Serbs to sign up to the deal. Even now, after weeks of bombing, the Russians and the G7 countries still maintain a common set of demands that the Serbs must meet. The fact which you do not wish to face is that every peaceful diplomatic alternative to war was tried and failed. Why? Because Milosevic gambled that we would fold. And you seem to wish that we had. The word for this is appeasement.

Yours,
Michael

May 1999

THE VIRTUAL COMMANDER

General Wesley K. Clark, speaking at a press conference at NATO's
Aviano air base, Italy, April 17, 1999.
(AP Photo/Franco Debernardi)

The Virtual Commander

Soon after the air war against Serbia began a NATO aircraft, probably an American F-15E Strike Eagle based at Aviano, Italy, came in high over the mountains above Pec, Kosovo's second city. Its target was a military communications tower located among a dozen Albanian houses laid out on an upland meadow above the city. About five miles from the tower, the 'wizzo' – the weapons system officer – released a laser-guided munition with a camera lens on the tip which homed in on the target. The strike – probably in total darkness – severed the tower's metal frame from its concrete base. Now the mangled frame lies on its side across a water-filled bomb crater, located just twenty-five feet from the homes of the Albanian families.

What separates a successful strike from a catastrophe is small – tiny, even – and illustrates the prodigious faith these modern acts of war imply: faith in technological 'systems' and in aviators three miles up, who have to distinguish between a military and a civilian target separated only by a dirt track.

Ever since the moment during the Gulf War in 1991 when reporters saw cruise missiles 'turning left at the traffic lights' to strike the bunkers of the Iraqi regime, the Western public has come to think of war like laser surgery. Displays of this kind of lethal precision at first awakened awe; now they are expected. We routinely demand perfection from the technology that surrounds us – our mobile phones, computers and cars. Why not war?

The task of managing this demand for perfection fell to General Wesley K. Clark, Supreme Allied Commander, Europe, or SACEUR. He may have a grand and imposing title, but he is a man with many masters: the nineteen nations who make up the NATO alliance and whose ambassadors sit on the North Atlantic Council, NATO's political decision-making body; Javier Solana, the Spanish Secretary-General of NATO who is responsible for keeping Clark's military operations under effective political control; and finally, and most important, as the commander of EUCOM, the American forces in Europe, Clark also answers to the Pentagon, the Joint Chiefs, the Secretary of Defense, and ultimately the President himself. The Americans supplied most of the intelligence as well as between sixty-five and eighty percent of the aircraft and the precision ordinance. The other NATO partners provided the rest of the air-crews and crucial political backing. Clark's job was to make coalition warfare work, to keep the high-precision equipment supplied by the Americans from being rendered ineffectual by the political and moral hesitations of nineteen allies running a war by committee. The war Clark found himself fighting wasn't exactly a war at all – it began without a formal declaration and it ended without complete victory – and it wasn't the one he would have fought had he been alone at the controls.

At various points in the campaign, the whisper went out that he was doing a bad job: too 'political,' too 'technocratic,' too 'weak,' too 'intense.' Perhaps he was only too candid. After the press conference on April 27 when he admitted that a month of bombing had not stopped the Serbs from reinforcing their troops in Kosovo, Clark was kept away from press briefings on orders from the Pentagon. The Administration feared he was hinting too openly that combat troops would be necessary if the air war failed. He didn't re-emerge at a press conference until June 12, to announce the entry of his troops into Kosovo. I met him two weeks later in his wood-panelled office at SHAPE – Supreme Headquarters, Allied Powers, Europe – in Mons, Belgium. He is a small, lithe, intense, thoughtful figure whose voice, with its soft Arkansas drawl, is unexpectedly gentle. He gives the impression of having strong emotions held under strict but not always perfect control.

Clark himself had entered Kosovo for the first time the day before. As he walked through the streets of Pristina, the people he had liberated chanted his name and pounded him on the back. On the television, the wiry grey-haired figure, jostled and sometimes dwarfed by the shouting Albanians, looked as exultant as a tightly-wired four-star general is ever likely to look.

Pristina must have been a moment to savor, but Clark wasn't celebrating much. Any euphoria he might have felt had evaporated when the Russian contingent beat his troops to Pristina airport. Clark had been forced to pretend publicly that it didn't matter at all, when in reality he was seething. *Newsweek* reported that he had wanted NATO troops to take the airport back from the Russians, and his commander on the ground, General Sir Mike Jackson, had replied that he wasn't going to take the world to the brink of World War III for the sake of an airfield in the southern Balkans. Altogether it had been a war unlike any other. Milosevic had withdrawn but he still had the power to do harm. Serb troops had left, but the UN administration had not yet arrived. At checkpoints on the roads in Kosovo, Clark's troops were occasionally taking and returning fire. The commander's mood was wary. 'I'm very watchful,' Clark said, speaking softly. 'There is no peace settlement. The ultimate division of political power has not been settled.'

The larger question was whether the air campaign – for all its astonishing accuracy – had actually worked. When the Serbian columns withdrew northwards in mid-June, with the men in sunglasses and bandannas standing up in the tanks making obscene gestures at the Western camera crews, it became clear that Clark's air campaign had not defeated Milosevic's forces in the field. It seemed strange that such a mighty display of air-power – 34,000 sorties over seventy-eight days – should have achieved such an ambiguous result. So if Milosevic had not been defeated militarily, why did he decide to withdraw? 'You'd have to ask Milosevic and he'll never tell you,' Clark replied.

The two men know each other about as well as enemies ever can. In 1995, Clark was the chief military liaison officer in the Holbrooke team at Dayton. In 1998 he delivered NATO's ultimatum to Milosevic to stop his repression in Kosovo and allow the entry of foreign monitors on the ground or face an air campaign. He knows what cigars the dictator smokes; he sat through his jokes and his tirades; he knows when he lies and when he tells the truth. Clark's staff will tell you that he did not conduct the war as a personal fight against Milosevic, but Clark's own briefings to the press – his choice of pronouns – tell a different story. It was not their air defense system that was hit, it was 'his' air defense system, 'his' tanks, 'his' petroleum and oil storage.

From the beginning Clark wanted to target Milosevic's bunkers, but NATO political leaders, for all their demonizing rhetoric, held back. It wasn't until the campaign was in its second month that Clark got approval to hit Milosevic's villa at Dobanovci, a Tito-era hunting preserve about thirty minutes from the center of Belgrade, set among forests and fields on the edge of a lake. It was there in September 1995, in the run-up to the Dayton accords, that Clark, Holbrooke and Milosevic shared a walk in the woods and Milosevic reminisced about his trips to New York as a Yugoslav state banker in the early 1980s. 'I want to smell that wonderful New York air again,' he told his American guests. On the porch at Dobanovci at a subsequent meeting, Milosevic suddenly suggested that the Americans might wish to meet Ratko Mladic, commander of Bosnian Serb forces and Radovan Karadjic, Bosnian Serb leader. While his Americans guests looked at each other in astonishment, Milosevic announced that the two men, Bosnia's most notorious war criminals, were just two hundred yards away in a nearby villa. Within minutes, they had sidled up to a porch and after a bitter late-night negotiating session, in which Milosevic broke the resistance of his Bosnian Serb clients, Clark and Holbrooke got the Serbs to lift the three-year siege of Sarajevo.

Clark never forgot the incident: that there must have been some kind of bunker, some kind of guest house, two hundred yards from Milosevic's front porch. Four years later, with the air war underway, Clark asked his aerial reconnaissance people to get him pictures from the unmanned drone aircraft patrolling the skies above Belgrade. Then he and his targeters pored over the images, zeroing in on Dobanovci and identifying the spot where Mladic and Karadjic had been holed up. Clark reasoned that this might be where Milosevic himself had gone to ground. 'Know what we did?' He raises his palm up, holds it there for a second and slams it down hard on the coffee table. Bam! The notebooks on his staffers' knees jump. 'We found it.' A flicker of raw exultation crosses his face.

But if Clark knew his enemy so well, why did he anticipate him so poorly? Why did he never imagine that Milosevic might respond to the air war by expelling most of a nation? Clark's intelligence people did envisage scenarios of possible ethnic cleansing, but the numbers they generated – 150,000-200,000 – fell woefully short of what the grand opportunist in Belgrade was prepared to unleash.

When the air campaign began, it was generally believed that a first wave of bombing would get Milosevic back to the negotiating table. And it was assumed that there would be a bombing pause after two days. Immediately, however, it became clear that 'strategic bombing lite' would not work.

In fact Clark had wanted a different approach from the outset. He and his air commanders, led by General Michael Short, a blunt, outspoken veteran of 276 combat missions in Vietnam, wanted to 'go downtown' on the first night, hitting the power, telephone, command-and-control sites and Milosevic's bunkers. But political leaders were holding the air-men back, ordering Clark to keep the strikes as light as possible. The politicians wouldn't approve strikes on occupied barracks, for example, for fear of causing too many casualties among conscripts. 'Basically, NATO's political sources were never happy with a phased air operation, because they wanted something more limited, more *diplomatique*.' Clark pronounces the last word with a crisp ironic edge.

NATO's initial confidence was misplaced. The Serbs were resisting: NATO pilots were encountering anti-aircraft and missile fire, and while they made it home, the aircraft were swerving and shuddering from the concussions of near misses. On the hillsides outside Aviano, Yugoslav amateur spotters, working with radio receivers were listening in to pilots on take-off and then using their cell phones to inform Belgrade of incoming strike patterns. Intelligence leaks from within NATO command may also have given the Serbs advance warning of the targets to be hit in the first phase of the campaign. A Stealth F-117 went down and though the aircrew was rescued, the aura of American air invincibility was shattered. Nor was NATO disabling Serb air defense. US radar-seeking missiles were unable to locate their targets because the Serbs were not activating their radar long enough for the missiles to lock on. Serb missile and anti-aircraft fire wasn't especially accurate, but it succeeded in keeping NATO planes above 15,000 feet.

At the end of March, with the politicians trying to micro-manage a campaign that was leading straight to failure, Clark obtained blanket approval from the North Atlantic Council, the supreme political body of the alliance, to go after broad categories of targets. At the same time, he called for reinforcements. The number of planes rose from four hundred to a thousand, drawn from thirteen member countries. Phase Two of the campaign – a ramped-up series of strikes on strategic targets in Serbia and forces in Kosovo – began on March 29.

Here was Clark, an army man, running a campaign he thought he couldn't win without ground troops. But President Clinton had ruled out ground options in the run up to the congressional elections in 1998, at a time when he was fighting for his political life. For other NATO countries too, like Greece and Italy, a ground war was politically impossible. Clark could not even go to the North Atlantic Council for formal authorization to begin planning one. Essentially, Clark was forced to prepare in secret for a ground operation, even as he himself declared that one was not in the offing.

Even now, Clark won't talk about these political con-straints. When asked whether the Allies should have positioned ground troops in Macedonia and Albania to put pressure on Milosevic, Clark parries the question with a shrug. 'I don't know whether Milosevic would have been impressed by the threat of ground troops. He obviously wasn't impressed by the threat of a NATO air operation.'

Not even his airmen were happy about going it alone, without a ground option. Clark knew that taking out tanks and artillery from the air broke with standard Air Force doctrine. Normally, pilots give close air support, going in only when their own troops are in contact with the enemy. 'It was sort of an unnatural act for air-men to fight a ground war without a ground component.'

In early April, with his political masters ruling out a ground option, Clark did the next best thing. He deployed the five-thousand-man Task Force Hawk to Albania, with twenty-four Apache helicopters. The move was as much a feint as anything else, designed to tie down Serb forces near the Albanian border and convince Milosevic that a ground option was in preparation. As it turned out, the helicopter pilots didn't have sufficient hours of flying time to be combat ready. Two machines went down and two pilots were killed. In any case, the Apaches were designed for combat support in a ground invasion, not as airborne attackers. But their mere presence in Albania kept Milosevic guessing. In the event, Task Force Hawk earned its keep not in combat, but through its target-acquisition radars positioned on the Albanian border. These radar systems peered into Kosovo and identified Serb artillery which was then pounded from the air.

Besides deploying Task Force Hawk to deceive Milosevic into believing a ground campaign was imminent, Clark had to improvise a much larger air campaign than he had ever intended. At the end of March he only had 100 approved targets, and he needed hundreds more. He also needed them fast: the standard Air Force tasking order – which assigns pilots to particular targets – took 72 hours to clear all its hurdles.

Clark had to develop a rapid reaction targeting system. Because he had no troops on the ground, there was no one to call in air strikes on to ground targets. Instead, Clark was forced to rely on airborne forward controllers, aloft in 30-year-old Lockheed EC 130 Es. He had to get their reaction times down so that they could spot and exploit targets of opportunity as they appeared on the radar screens. He went to his air force commanders – men like Michael Short and Daniel Leaf, at Aviano – and at first they didn't understand what he wanted. They told him, give us the targets, and we'll take them out. He recalls replying, 'You don't get it. *You* develop the targets.' But we don't do that, his commanders replied. 'So we had to fix that,' he says tersely. And they did. Clark's team improvised a computerized, real-time target development and review process which pulled together American and NATO intelligence assets, the force commanders in Italy, Macedonia and Albania and the battle planners and targeters at Clark's headquarters in Belgium. No such system existed at the beginning of the war, and it wasn't fully operational until late April. But when it had been cobbled together, it gave Clark control of his air war.

Every morning planners at American bases in Italy, Germany, Belgium and the United States logged on to the SIPERNET, the US military's secure digitalized network and began putting together target folders – slides with aerial reconnaissance pictures of a target, assessments of its military significance and a grading for possible collateral damage. Data specialists at EUCOM's Joint Analysis Centre in Molesworth, England, fed the system targets picked up by the Predator and Hunter unmanned drone aircraft, being used for the first time to photograph targets. Weapons experts at the Combined Allied Operations Center in Vicenza, Italy – an agglomeration of windowless prefabs and containers crammed with screens and computers, and the operational center for the air war – would then select the most appropriate ordnance types for the target and Clark's targeters at SHAPE would evaluate the designated mean point of impact or DMPI ('dimpy') according to four grades of collateral damage.

Legal and moral evaluation of the target was also built into the computerized operation. At a base in Germany, a military lawyer from the Judge Advocate General's office, sitting at his computer screen, would assess the target in terms of the Geneva Conventions governing the laws of war. He would rule whether it was a justifiable military objective in legal terms and whether its value outweighed the potential costs in collateral damage. A military lawyer also applied 'the reasonable person standard' of judgment to the fine line separating military and civilian targets.

Because of these legal constraints, the pilot's rules of engagement were strict, 'as strict as I have seen in twenty-seven years,' in the opinion of General Chuck Wald who helped co-ordinate the approval of targets with the Joint Chiefs in the Pentagon. Pilots could only fire on visual recognition of a target – which meant that bad weather forced many sortie cancel-lations – and they often had to radio in to the air war headquarters at Vicenza for a final approval when they saw a target of opportunity. In mid-May General Short told *The New York Times* that his pilots would call him directly if they weren't sure. ' "Boss, I see village and I see tanks parked next to the houses in the village. What do you want me to do?" And I'll say, "Tell them to hit the tanks." And if he hits a house by mistake, that's my responsibility.'

Even so, with all the controls in place, with all the precision weaponry, the final decisions were up to young pilots searching for their 'dimpy' through two 4.5-inch by 4.5-inch target monitors. They made judgments which they will live with for the rest of their lives: believing that the trucks on the road to Djakovica on April 14 were a military convoy and discovering too late that they might have been a tractor-load of refugees; pressing the trigger to release ammunition against a bridge and discovering at the last second that a train was crossing it. The pilots' identities were shielded from the press, so it was Clark himself who went out after the bridge bombing, and showed the press the horrible gun camera footage: how the weapon was released and a passenger train came into view, a split-second too late.

As commander-in-chief, Clark's contact with the war, apart

from flying visits to the pilots at Aviano and the troops in Macedonia and Albania, was virtual rather than visceral. The two fixed points of his war were VTCs – video teleconference meetings – held every morning in secure rooms in SHAPE headquarters. These command centers are more corporate than military in appearance, low-ceilinged rooms with two ranks of desks for advisers flanking the commander's console which faces a 54-inch video screen.

At 9 a.m. Clark would conduct his first VTC, with the NATO force leaders. They would review the results of the previous day's bombings and go over timelines for the coming day. Intelligence officers and targeters would flash targeting slides up on the screen and discuss them. Any NATO country that had pilots or planes in the air on a proposed target also had to give approval, and Clark often had to call Paris or Bonn to get European politicians or chiefs of staff to agree to a particular strike. One American officer who sat in on these meetings said they involved agonizing horse-trading. When Clark found himself blocked politically, he would ring up Javier Solana, the NATO Secretary-General and say, 'You've got to help me with target 183. I need 183.' And Solana would go to work on the member state that was objecting.

This was the price of coalition warfare, and the only way to make it work was to split the targeting process in two. After the NATO teleconference, Clark would go down to another briefing room for a VTC with EUCOM. All operations using American assets – such as planes with stealth technology or cruise missiles – were managed not through the NATO chain of command but through EUCOM. At this meeting, Clark would sign off on targets and pass them on to the Joint Chiefs in Washington, who would send particularly sensitive targets to the White House for clearance – approval usually came within 30 minutes.

Clark kept the coalition from paralyzing the air war by keeping NATO out of missions using American planes. At Vicenza there were two completely separate targeting teams, called cells, one for NATO warplanes, the other strictly American assets. Fearing – rightly as it turned out – that other NATO countries might leak target information to the Serbs, America was parsimonious in sharing intelligence and targeting information with its allies. Even the British, who were America's closest allies, were not fully informed of American strike targets and intentions. The USAF kept its key strike aircraft – the B-2 bomber – based in Whiteman Air Force base in Missouri so that its own allies would not snoop around its advanced and highly secret stealth technology.

The computerized target system was pulling all Clark's intelligence assets together but it had one blindingly obvious failing. As Clark called for ever more targets and these, now numbering a thousand possibles, were turned into target folders, nobody thought to question the accuracy of target designation. The target folders looked so plausible: a recon-naissance photo, data on military significance, gradings for possible collateral damage – no one questioned whether all this virtual data corresponded to anything real.

That was essentially how Wes Clark's worst moment of the war came about – the bombing of the Chinese Embassy on May 7. Judging from the look that comes over his face when he talks about it, the strike was definitely an accident. 'That was a real stunner,' he said quietly. Alastair Campbell, Blair's Press Secretary, confirms that the strike was just as much of a surprise to Downing Street. American intelligence was picking up Serbian military signals emanating from the site – why they still do not know – and when the target was sent for identification at the CIA, it was wrongly designated as a storage or logistics facility. Mid-level CIA analysts who warned that the target had been misidentified couldn't get their message into the targeting process in time. The maps were old, the identification two years out of date. Appalled at the diplomatic consequences, which seemed to sink any chance of Chinese approval of a UN resolution to end the conflict, the NATO ambassadors and heads of government told Clark to re-check every target identification and err on the side of caution. There was no recurrence, but the myth of error-free war had been destroyed.

Political micromanagement continued throughout the campaign. After the war was over, President Chirac of France boasted to a French reporter that if there were bridges still standing in Belgrade, it was thanks to him. Clark was never allowed to forget what was at stake for the politicians. Tony Blair did leave the show to Wes Clark but he came to Clark's office and told him straight out that the political future of every leader in Europe depended on the outcome. 'Are you in this to win?' Blair asked him. Clark said he was.

Containing and deflecting these political pressures was the essence of Clark's war. While his commanders were bridling at what they saw as interference, Clark, a political animal to his core, managed to finesse and soothe the anxieties of his political masters while keeping them from running the campaign. His political instincts told him he had to keep aircrew losses to a minimum because headlines announcing yet another downed plane would have brought the campaign to a close within days. But, he went on, 'I never expected to get zero'.

By keeping pilot loss near zero, he kept the campaign going. But progress on the targets was agonizingly slow and Clark knew he had to deliver. By early May, hawks in the editorial columns were questioning Clark's supposed decision to keep the pilots above 15,000 feet. In reality, pilots frequently flew below the 15,000-foot ceiling, but soon discovered, in Clark's words, that 'flying low doesn't pay.' Pilots breaking out below cloud formations in the middle of mountainous terrain at five hundred knots could focus only on keeping airborne. The simple reality was that, high or low, the pilots were having little impact on the ethnic cleansing. The senior US aviator, Brigadier General Daniel Leaf, experiencing his first combat missions under fire in his F-16, could see it happening below. 'I could actually see them burning houses. It was extraordinary and horrifying.'

Clark's fliers were frustrated by their inability to hit Serb forces in the field. The Serbs proved to be expert at camouflage, deception and the use of decoys. They built fake bridges and applied heat-reflecting camouflage paint to the real ones so as to throw off the target acquisition radars. Pilots would strike what they thought was a tank and watch an inflatable rubber decoy deflate like a pricked balloon. Clark was visibly nettled during one press conference when Martin Walker, a correspondent for the *Guardian*, asked him why NATO was using million-dollar weapons to take out ten-thousand-dollar targets. But this was exactly what was happening: high-cost precision ordinance was being thrown at aging Soviet artillery and tanks, and more often than not, failing to take them out. The only troops on the ground capable of calling in fire against Serb forces on the ground were KLA units in the mountainous regions along the Albanian border. NATO did not want to be the KLA's air force and did not integrate them into the American target acquisition and identification process. They were not given weapons and although local commanders did get on to their cell phones and call up American contacts to identify the locations of Serb troops, they were denied the communications equipment necessary to serve as forward air controllers for the planes overhead.

The KLA engaged the Serb forces around Mt. Pastric in the last week of May and first week of June and drew Serb forces out of their positions, exposing them to attack from the air. This led KLA sources to claim that air power became effective only when it was teamed with ground forces supplied by the KLA. Clark's targeteers are skeptical of KLA claims. The Albanian fighters exaggerated their own military impact, and German troops who have looked around the Mt. Pastric battlefield, once the Serbs withdrew, were unable to find the tanks and artillery pieces of military units which the KLA claimed to have exposed to destruction from the air.

The hard fact is that the mightiest air forces in the world were unable to destroy Milosevic's army in the field. Clark himself insists that his airmen took out 100 tanks, 210 armored fighting vehicles, and 449 artillery and mortar tubes. But the numbers themselves don't prove much. General Leaf, who flew eighteen F-16 missions during the war, argued fiercely on the phone from his base at Aviano, Italy, that 'counting tanks is irrelevant. The fact is they withdrew and while they took tanks with them, they returned to a country whose military infrastructure has been ruined. They're not going to be doing anything with those forces for a long time.' The air campaign did drive the Serbs into dugouts, bunkers and revetments to escape the B-52s overhead. A tank hidden underground, Leaf argued, is not much use to anybody. If the demonstrations by reservists in southern Serbia, refusing to go back to the front, are any indication, the Serbian casualty rate was also increasing in the last week of the war.

Still, despite overwhelming superiority, NATO never ruled the skies over Kosovo. The Serbs proved agile at husbanding their air defense resources, moving missile sites and radar systems around to evade strikes, being careful not to turn on their radars in order to attract fire. The Serbs had talked to the Iraqis and the Iraqis had told them, in Clark's words, 'turn on that radar and you're dead meat.' Serbs managed to keep firing at NATO planes till the last day of the war.

By late May, both Clark and NATO's political leaders were desperate for results. A string of dreadful accidents – hitting the train on the bridge, bombing the refugee convoy and a strike against a Serbian old people's home – were all draining away public support for the air war. Opinion polls were shifting alarmingly. The campaign's mistakes – rare as they were – were consuming its legitimacy. There were perhaps only ten days of viable, i.e. politically acceptable, targets left.

At this point, Clark finally secured approval for the key strikes of the war. At the beginning of May his aircraft had hit the transformer yards of the Yugoslav power grid with graphite bombs. They were so-called 'clean' strikes, causing the transformer yards to short out rather than disabling the generators themselves. Lights in major cities went out for between eight and twenty-four hours. When the Serbs got the system back on line, the yards were hit again, and again the system went down temporarily. Finally, on 24 May, heavier munitions took the grid out completely. Hitting these yards turned out to be the single most effective military strike of the campaign. Everything from the computers which run a country's banking system to the systems which operate air-defense radar stations depends on the grid. Hitting it also sent a powerful message to the civilian population. Until the grid strikes, as Clark put it, 'this was the only air campaign in history in which lovers strolled down river banks in the gathering twilight and ate out at outdoor cafés and watched the fireworks.' After the grid was destroyed, both the political elite and the people knew that NATO had secured control of the regime's central nervous system.

The extraordinary fact about the air war was that it was more effective against civilian infrastructure than against forces in the field. The irony here was obvious: the most effective strike of the war was also the most problematic. Hitting the grid meant taking out the power to hospitals, babies' incubators, water-pumping stations. The lawyers made this clear to Clark. As one of them recalled, 'We'd have preferred not to have to take on these targets. But this was the Commander's call.' Once the power went off in Belgrade the regime's days were numbered: its command and control structure was disrupted, and such civilian support as it had began to ebb away.

Despite political bickering behind the scenes over target selection, the aircrews of the NATO countries who did fly the combined missions over Serbia actually made coalition warfare work – at the speed of sound and in the dark. Leaf recalled leading his F-16 into a night attack on a Belgrade area petroleum storage depot and realizing that there was a Dutch fighter on one wing-tip engaged in suppressing the Serb MiG 29s, a German fighter beside him firing Harm missiles at the Serb radars and an Italian plane flying combat air patrol overhead. All of them were wearing night vision goggles; all of them were observing total radio silence, and all of them returned to base with their mission accomplished.

Night vision goggles – only in use with NATO pilots for the last eighteen months or so – were perhaps the key new innovation in the war. They gave NATO ownership of the night. The goggles look like opera glasses and are attached by a clip to a pilot's helmet. He flips them down like a baseball outfielder flicking down his shades to make a catch in the sun. The effect, say the pilots, is stunning. Look out of the cockpit without the glasses, and all you see is blackness. Flip down the glasses and you see an F-16 on your wing-tip.

For all its technical sophistication, the air campaign might have turned out very differently if the Russians had given the Serbs their latest technology. The air war was essentially a duel between Seventies Soviet air defense technology and state-of-the-art American precision-guidance systems. If NATO had been up against Eighties Soviet technology, it might have lost twenty planes, and it is unclear that NATO electorates would have stood such losses. The key to a successful outcome was American diplomatic leverage on the Russians. Deputy Secretary of State Strobe Talbott has confirmed that the US 'repeatedly and explicitly' warned Russia not to provide Yugoslavia with 'any military assistance – matériel, know-how, personnel.' 'We didn't mince words,' as he put it. Any Russian assistance which increased risk to US pilots would have had a 'devastating' effect on the future of US-Russian relations.

Diplomacy, in other words, was just as important in changing Milosevic's mind as the air war. He gambled that Russia would support him, and that their support would cause the NATO alliance to fracture. In the event, it didn't. For all their talk of Slavic brotherhood, the Russians decided that their ultimate national interest lay with America, not with a Balkan dictator. Herein lies another major irony. If Russia had been what Western policy-makers had wanted it to be for a decade – i.e. a functioning pluralist democracy – it would not have behaved as the West wanted it to. A democratic Russia would have supported the Serbs more actively. Yeltsin the autocrat was able to ignore popular feeling in favor of Serbia and instruct Chernomyrdin to abandon the Milosevic regime. That he did so, senior American officials believe, was due to the channel of communication between Vice-President Gore and Chernomyrdin, established when the latter was Prime Minister of Russia.

Gore apparently warned Chernomyrdin of what allied intelligence already knew about Milosevic's war crimes, and forced the Russians to ask themselves whether they wanted to associate themselves with massacre. When Judge Louise Arbour, the chief prosecutor of the International Tribunal at the Hague, indicted Milosevic for war crimes on May 27 some State Department circles feared it would make a diplomatic solution more difficult. It reality it made it impossible for the Russians to turn back. The diplomatic encirclement of the Milosevic regime was complete, just as the strikes against the grid finally convinced him that the price of his gamble had become too high. At the last moment, military force and diplomatic leverage came together.

Clark was the architect of the air war, not of the diplomacy which actually brought it to an end. But he never lost sight of the curious fact that his war was not a war at all, but an exercise in coercive diplomacy designed to change one man's mind.

Now that the planes are back in their hangars, what is striking about the conflict is the disconnection between the high moral language of the cause and the limited character of the war itself. The political leaders of NATO talked the language of ultimate commitment and practiced the warfare of minimum risk. As commander, Clark was placed in an often impossible position: being asked to wage a war that was clean yet lethal, just yet effective, moral yet ruthless. The paradox is that greater ruthlessness – going downtown on the first night and taking out the grid – might have been more effective, and in the end, more merciful.

Clausewitz would have called Kosovo a cabinet war. Unlike a total war – and the Gulf War was the last of these – the Kosovo war did not mobilize hundreds of thousands of men. It mobilized opinion around the world, but it was fought by no more than 1,500 NATO airmen, and the elite specialists of Serbian air defense, probably numbering no more than a thousand. It was fought in VTC conference rooms, using target folders flashed up on a screen, and all that a commander like Clark ever saw of the rush of battle was the gun camera footage e-mailed every night on secure internet systems to his headquarters in Belgium. Cabinet wars are fought and won by technicians and Clark's team produced a virtuoso display of technical improvisation. Cabinet wars do not end with parades, garlands, civic receptions or sorrowful ceremonies at grave-yards. They do not reach deep into the psyche of a people; they do not demand blood and sacrifice and they do not reward their heroes. The campaign took its cool, enclosed and disciplined commander to his outer limits: in terms of stamina, political acumen, will-power and leadership. But there will be no ticker-tape parade for Wesley K. Clark. It was not that kind of war. No sooner was it completed than his political masters in the

Pentagon, led by Defense Secretary William Cohen, decided to replace him with an airforce general less likely to argue back. The man who won the first postmodern war in history was now looking for a job.

June 1999

JUSTICE AND REVENGE

Louise Arbour visiting a village where a mass grave had been
discovered, July 14, 1999.
(Photo © Daher/GAMMA)

Justice and Revenge, July 1999

Celine is a small village on the road between Prizren and Djakovica in western Kosovo. It is a hot July morning and about a hundred villagers are waiting for a helicopter to land in the meadow beside what remains of the local school. It has been torched: the roof timbers are lying among charred children's desks. The red and black Kosovo flag flies over the ruins.

A clutch of brown-faced schoolchildren are standing against a rope line, holding bunches of wilting flowers picked from their family's gardens. They have been told that an important woman is coming to see them. They do not know who she is, but they like the idea that she is coming in a helicopter and so they peer up into the sky and cock their ears for the sound of rotor blades.

The older men of the village sit on the meadow grass in a circle, smoking, running their fingers through their mustaches and staring at the mountains across the valley. They are wearing the *kelesche*, the conical cap of Albanian country people. The women, in their best white embroidered dresses and kerchiefs, sit in a separate circle, talking among themselves. One of them wipes away tears with the back of her hand.

As the sun rises in the sky, camera crews begin to arrive: young people in wraparound sunglasses, shorts, T-shirts and Caterpillar boots. They are from CNN, Reuters, Sky and Channel Four Television from London, plus the *Washington Post*, National Public Radio, and Deutsche Welle.

About forty yards from the cameras and reporters, on the other side of rope line, there is a Dutch armored personnel carrier with signalers inside talking on the radio phone. Next to the APC are a couple of military tents with camouflage nets spread between them. Inside one of the tents, a heavy-set man in white shirt and chinos is poring over a map. He looks glumly at the gathering of the TV crews, lights a cigarette and comes out to talk to them. His name is Bill Gent and he is a senior officer with London's Metropolitan Police. He is in charge of the forensic team – pathologists, archeologists, anthropologists, ballistics specialists – who are digging in the ravine behind Celine.

After a long wait, a Huey with German markings comes up over the hill behind the village, circles twice and settles down gently beside the school, while Dutch soldiers positioned on the perimeter duck and shield their faces from the rotor blast. A short female figure wearing black glasses, her shoulders hunched and head bowed, steps down from the helicopter and, with a small entourage following behind, approaches the villagers, gathering against the rope line.

Louise Arbour doesn't like scenes like this: she is a criminal prosecutor, not a celebrity, yet she plunges into what the scene requires, taking the bouquets held out by the children, stroking their cheeks, clasping some of the hands held out to her and saying over and over: 'Thank you, thank you.'

Kosovo has been in NATO's hands for a month. Since then, the troops, together with Arbour's investigators from the International Tribunal at the Hague have been finding 'sites' everywhere. The whole of Kosovo, she has been quoted as saying, was 'one vast crime scene.' She had been up in the French sector that morning at Mitrovica and next she will be visiting a site near Gnilane where the Canadian RCMP is digging; now she wants to see what her team has found at Celine. She gets into Bill Gent's Land Rover and they drive down the hill, followed by the reporters' jeeps. The villagers stay where they are: they know what there is to see. But the crews don't: they push and shove each other to get a shot of Louise Arbour looking down into the pit and slowly shaking her head.

I do not go down in the ravine – I know what is there. So I wait for her to return. When she comes back up to the forensic team's tent, she does not look shocked or dismayed, just tired. The crowd is about fifty yards away, watching her every move. While she has not said she will bring them truth and justice, that is what they expect. I ask her whether these isn't something cruel about these expectations. How likely is it that she or anyone else will find the men who killed the villagers of Celine – twenty-one of them – for no other reason than that they were Kosovar Albanians? She thinks about this, hands on hips, head down, and then says fiercely: 'We have no choice. We owe it to these people. If there are expectations, we just have to meet them.'

They are calling her over to the rope line, and she duly goes

117

and shakes hands, and bows her head in thanks, and then her staff turns her towards the helicopter – rotors now whirring up the dust – and she climbs aboard, and is suddenly airborne, whirling overhead. A tiny hand is just visible waving down at us, and then the chopper wheels around and vanishes behind the next hill.

I had been to talk to Louise Arbour in Holland in mid-June. Her office at the International Criminal Tribunal for the former Yugoslavia (ICTY) – where she has served as Chief Prosecutor since 1996 – is on the second floor corner of a former insurance building in the Dutch capital, the Hague. She is also Chief Prosecutor for the Tribunal on Rwanda, sitting in Arusha, Tanzania. The two tribunals were created in 1993 and 1994 by Western governments who had done little or nothing to stop the crimes these tribunals were set up to punish. Instead of armed intervention, the international community promised the victims justice, in the form of a prosecutor, a panel of judges and a secretariat of investigators and lawyers.

She has two secretaries in the outer office, but her door is open, and she wanders in and out, wearing slacks and a blouse and sensible flat shoes. When she wants to give me a copy of a speech she rummages around for it herself in her secretary's filing cabinet.

As for her appearance, French words apply: she is *petite* and *soignée*, feminine, Québecoise, amusing, worldly-wise and business-like without appearing relentless. She has become a famous person, but she seems to wear this lightly. In press conferences, you occasionally see her look over the tops of her bifocals and fix a journalist with a withering gaze. Then she can seem formidable. But her staff do not appear to go in fear of her.

Today, there is laughter in the outer office, an easy feeling that things are going well. And for good reason.

On May 27, three weeks before we met, she had indicted Slobodan Milosevic, President of the Federal Republic of Yugoslavia, along with five of his associates for war crimes committed in Kosovo since January 1, 1999. It was the first indictment for war crimes of a sitting head of state. Now that NATO had entered Kosovo and Milosevic was an international pariah everyone seemed to think the indictment was an excellent idea, but that was not what anonymous briefers in foreign capitals, especially Washington, had been whispering when the war was still going on. Then, 'State department sources' had been telling journalists that the indictment would jeopardize the negotiations for a settlement. Now, of course, everyone was lining up to take the credit.

When we sit down to talk across the desk in her office, I ask her directly about her independence as a prosecutor, especially whether she had control over the timing of the indictment. She insists that the timing was entirely up to her. 'Nobody gave us this case,' she says defiantly, meaning NATO. Yet her relationship with NATO is ambiguous. Officially, of course, it has nothing to do with her office. Practically, of course, Arbour is dependent on NATO governments for everything from the helicopters that fly her to the sites in Kosovo to the secret intelligence she needed in order to indict Milosevic.

If NATO didn't determine the timing of the indictment, what about the UN? Her mandate is from the UN Security Council. Did the permanent five – especially the Americans – have a say in the timing? Absolutely not, she insists. Her instructions are clear. 'The Security Council didn't say go out and investigate and then come back for instructions. They said, "Go to the top, investigate and when you have the evidence, you shall indict. End of discussion."' When she says this, she doesn't look like someone who brooks much disagreement.

When I ask her whether she thinks her indictment helped to end the war, by convincing the Russians to abandon the Serbs and convincing Milosevic that the game was up, she shrugs and laughs. 'We weren't going to take the blame (if the negotiations failed) and now we would like to take the credit – but you can't have it both ways.'

The Milosevic indictment is several hundred pages thick and its contents are secret. Arbour presented the sealed document to Judge David Anthony Hunt of Australia, one of the sitting judges of the International Tribunal. His scrutiny was the first test she had to pass. After a weekend poring over the dossier, Hunt ruled not merely that the case could proceed, but that the evidence 'if uncontradicted' by defense attorneys was sufficient to ensure conviction. Milosevic is now rumored to have retained defense counsel, though the prospect of him ever surrendering to the Hague to face trial seems remote. Even if he never faces trial, however, indictment has weighty consequences: his foreign assets are frozen; his international bank accounts can be subpoenaed; and he cannot travel. His kingdom – Serbia – has become his prison.

The Serbian leader has been so comprehensively demonized in the Western press that it is easy to forget that the outcome of a trial – if it ever should come – would hardly be a foregone conclusion. Linking a head of state to sordid murders, committed by hands unknown, in tiny Kosovar villages hundreds of miles from his capital is far from simple. The mere fact that Milosevic was head of state and commander-in-chief of the forces responsible for the killings is not enough. Beyond *de jure* responsibility, Arbour has to prove direct *de facto* authorization from Milosevic for specific atrocities. The indictment actually lists the villages in which massacres occurred – not Celine itself, but next door and down the road – and names the persons, 340 of them, whose deaths she seeks to attribute to Milosevic directly. Milosevic's probable defense is that a head of state cannot be held responsible either for the excesses of those under his direct orders, or, still less, for freelance paramilitaries not under his formal command. Judge Hunt wouldn't have approved the indictment without detailed evidence, rebutting both of these points. So what is in the indictment?

When Arbour stonewalls, is it an impressive performance. I get nowhere. 'Why should I give the defense any clues?' she says with a sharp smile and a flick of her hand.

Nailing down Milosevic's command responsibility depended on military intelligence: satellite imagery, photographs from NATO's unarmed drone aircraft, radio communication intercepts and data from 'physical assets' – agents on the ground. If you believe the Serbian version of events – which makes the Tribunal a kind of judicial accomplice of the NATO bombing – all Arbour had to do was ask NATO for the intelligence she needs. In fact, NATO itself only warehouses intelligence and General Wesley Clark could not authorize its release. The real work of intelligence-gathering is done in individual national capitals, who jealously guard ownership of their data. In January and February, she toured them all, starting with Bonn, pleading for co-operation. The Germans, who operated drone aircraft over Kosovo, gave her some pictures of grave sites. The Austrians also listen in to Yugoslav telecommunications. It was the Germans and the Austrians, apparently, who provided Arbour with evidence of 'Operation Horseshoe,' the Serbian master plan – developed in the autumn of 1998 and authorized by Milosevic early in 1999 – for a semi-circular sweep of Kosovo by army and paramilitary groups which drove most of the population of Kosovo into Albania and Macedonia in late March. The British also supplied Arbour with intelligence intercepts from their central monitoring and listening post in Cheltenham.

But only the Americans – with the satellites, high-flying manned spy planes, unmanned drones, and other electronic eavesdropping devices – had the resources to listen in to the heartbeat of the Serbian regime, the commands issued by Milosevic to his armed forces, paramilitaries and military police. Arbour knew that if she was ever going to indict Milosevic, she would have to get the assistance of the tentacular American 'intelligence community' – the CIA, FBI, the Defense Intelligence Agency, and the National Security Agency.

Their initial reactions – from 1993 to 1997 – had been negative. When investigating war crimes committed in Bosnia, Arbour and her predecessor in the prosecutor's job, Judge Richard Goldstone of South Africa's Constitutional Court, were denied the intelligence co-operation necessary to link Milosevic to the Bosnian Serb chain of command. American intelligence regards all international bodies – even NATO – as sieves. These suspicions weren't without foundation: it was a French NATO officer, after all, who had leaked to the Serbs the plans for an air war drawn up in the event that Richard Holbrooke's negotiations with Milosevic on Kosovo in October 1998 had failed. During the war itself, targeting data was leaked to the Serbs. Now a Canadian judge, based in the Hague, was asking them for some of the most sensitive information on their computers. Even worse, she actually wanted to 'task' their sources – for example, to assign a drone aircraft to take pictures of a suspected massacre site on a particular day. At first the Americans balked.

When Arbour took over the prosecutor's job in August 1996, she wasn't allowed to even discuss imagery with her intelligence community sources. But in 1997, US Secretary of State Madeleine Albright nominated David Scheffer as her special representative on war crimes issues, and after what he describes, circumspectly, as 'labour intensive' negotiations between the State Department and the intelligence community, he began to make some impact in getting the intelligence community to release confidential data to Arbour. There was never a flood of material, just a steady trickle. By April 1999, she and her staff were poring over satellite imagery, some of it tasked to suit their purposes. The case against Milosevic was coming together, but it still lacked crucial evidence of Milosevic's direct commands to his troops in the field. This was the smoking gun: and it could only come from telecommunications intercepts. Without it, the indictment would rely on the *de jure* paper chain of command linking Milosevic to the men in ski-masks and that would not have been enough.

The *Washington Post* has claimed that the timing of the indictment was determined by the Americans' delivery of crucial intercepts in the last week of May. Scheffer denies this, and so does Arbour. There was no last minute gusher of data which determined the timing. Moreover, the data which was supplied wasn't sufficient to establish Arbour's case. Scheffer, when reached at his office in the State Department in Washington, said that intelligence data merely 'points the prosecutor in the right direction.' It is up to her, he said, 'to make the case.' It can be inferred that American intelligence knew more than they let her have and she had to frame an indictment with several pieces of the puzzle still missing. When asked whether Arbour did get everything she needed, Scheffer asks a rhetorical question of his own: 'Is the customer ever satisfied?' When Scheffer's own team finally read the text of Arbour's indictment, their reaction was – in Scheffer's own words – 'This is just the beginning. There's a lot more out there.' Which means that the Milosevic indictment, as it currently stands, is just a skeleton: more charges will follow, not just in relation to Kosovo, but also in relation to the war in Bosnia.

Both Scheffer and Arbour concur on one point. It was she, not the Americans, who made the indictment happen. Scheffer puts it this way: 'the indictment was not made in the USA.'

During the war, whenever Arbour appeared in photos with General Wesley Clark or British Foreign Secretary Cook, the impression was created of the prosecutor being NATO's judicial arm. Journalists believed this and kept asking Arbour whether she was under pressure from London and Washington to bring down an indictment soon. She laughs when she remembers this: 'I find it ironic that many journalists asked me: Are you being pressured? It became very clear the only message I was getting in all of these capitals was one of total ambivalence and ambiguity. Not: Do it now, or do it later, or don't do it. If I try to articulate what I was being told, I was being told: NOTHING.'

As for the Americans, David Scheffer was obviously in favor of a speedy indictment, but other power sources in the State

Department (like Deputy Secretary Strobe Talbott, in charge of the delicate negotiations with Yeltsin's special envoy, Victor Chernomyrdin) feared that an indictment might jeopardize a diplomatic end to the bombing. There were still others, like Richard Holbrooke, who envisaged the possibility that the bombing would fail to break Milosevic's will, and that the US would have to do a direct deal with the Serbian leader. It was to forestall this possibility – a Houdini-like diplomatic escape by Milosevic – that Arbour brought down her indictment on May 27.

As long as the indictment remains sealed, everyone can take the credit, including those who actually didn't give her any help at all. 'The minute we get these accused into the dock,' Arbour says now, 'it will be very clear what we have and where we got it from. Those people who want to take credit prematurely should be careful.' She laughs. The record will speak for itself, who blinked first, who were the good guys first. The story is all going to be there.'

She is proud of what she did – proud of her staff too – for establishing the credibility and legitimacy of her office. She knows that the Tribunal itself was established in 1993 by Western governments in a temporary fit of guilt as a substitute for doing something serious to stop the ethnic cleansing in Bosnia. Both she and her predecessor Judge Goldstone turned an institution which had no real precedent in international law and precious little backing from Western governments, into what Arbour calls 'a real time law enforcement agency.' In the process they both discovered the huge gap that separates what Western states preach about human rights from what they actually practice.

When Arbour arrived at the Hague in the late summer of

1996, there were only seven suspects in custody. Bosnia had been partitioned according to the Dayton agreement and the NATO troops patrolling each of the sectors were not tasked to arrest war criminals. The commander of NATO troops, Admiral Leighton Smith, maintained that arrests weren't part of his mandate. Wanted criminals like Radovan Karadjic had driven straight through NATO checkpoints. Without arrested indictees the tribunal would be out of business.

It took a year, and a change of government in Britain, for the Bosnia contingents to begin tracking down war crimes suspects. In August 1997 – on direct orders from Tony Blair's incoming Labour government – British soldiers swooped inside the Serbian enclave in Bosnia and arrested suspects wanted in connection with the notorious concentration camp at Prijedor where Bosnian Muslims had been raped, tortured and killed in the summer of 1992. These arrests were the turning point in the Tribunal's history: now it has a full pen of suspects awaiting trial and more arrests nearly every week. Arbour smiles broadly when she recalls the moment of those arrests, and she clearly longs to tell the story of the secret diplomacy which brought it about. But 'I can't. I won't,' she says. However the outline of the story is clear: basically, she shamed Western governments into recognizing that if they didn't allow the arrest of suspected war criminals, the Tribunal process would dry up, she would resign and those governments' commitments to the Tribunal would be exposed as a sham.

Making the arrests in Bosnia, bringing a stream of indictees into detention in the Hague saved the Tribunal from a slow death. The next task was to establish the Tribunal's authority over national governments. Although the Tribunal had been in business for three years by the time she arrived, governments thought that co-operation with its subpoenas was voluntary. Arbour took a look at the Security Council's mandate and thought differently. 'The assumption everywhere – including my office – was that all we were entitled to was co-operation. But you can't run a criminal justice system as a charity. Read the statute: states shall co-operate and shall comply with orders. A subpoena is an order. You get one. You show up. End of story.'

When she took the government of Croatia to court in the Hague to force it to hand over one of its indictees, Tihomir Blaskic, the gallery of the court was crowded with diplomats because the precedent was obvious: if Arbour forced Croatia to co-operate, then all states would have to follow suit. Arbour won the Blaskic ruling, and it changed the mood in her office. Although Croatia, like Serbia, still defies Arbour, the Tribunal has become more aggressive in defending its jurisdiction. 'Everybody stopped whining, saying there's no political will, no one helps us. All of a sudden we started to have a self-perception which was accurate. We have a huge amount of power.'

More power, in fact, than anyone including NATO, quite realizes. All through the Kosovo war, Arbour kept waiting for reporters to ask her whether she had jurisdiction over the pilots flying the bombing missions. Nobody ever did. In fact, the wording of the Security Council mandate is clear: the Tribunal has jurisdiction over every combatant in the former Yugoslavia irrespective of citizenship. That includes the American, Canadian, British, Dutch, Spanish, French and Portuguese pilots who flew the F-15s over Serbia. By initiating air operations over Yugoslavia, NATO countries, especially America, brought themselves within the jurisdiction of an international tribunal which they thought applied only to Balkan peoples.

When I tell her I have been talking to American military lawyers about the Tribunal, she leans forward, 'And what do they say? Do they accept our jurisdiction?'

American air-force lawyers, attached to the American European Command express themselves cagily. Yes, in theory, they concede, Arbour has jurisdiction over our pilots. In practice, they say, we'd never give them jurisdiction. Any pilot accused of a war crime would be flown home and tried under the American uniform code of military justice. So if Milosevic's Serbia continues to deny the Tribunal's jurisdiction, so – in practice, if not in theory – do the Americans.

This is part of a larger pattern. The Hague and Arusha Tribunals are temporary institutions set up by the Security Council and their mandates expire when the Council deems that they have done their job. Ever since Nuremberg, there have been calls to establish a permanent tribunal, an international criminal court (ICC) to try the crimes of waging aggressive war, war crimes, genocide and crimes against humanity. While Canada and other Western countries have supported the ICC, America led the opposition that whittled away its powers and jurisdiction. Arbour herself has done a critique of the limitations of the ICC, pointing out that, as drafted, any nation can pre-empt an international criminal prosecution of one of their nationals simply by initiating a national criminal trial of their own. That means, in effect, that the powers she exercises as an international prosecutor at the Hague are unlikely to be reproduced in the permanent International Tribunal.

David Scheffer, who leads the American delegation on the creation of the ICC, disagrees, pointing out that according to the draft statute of the ICC the Security Council could refer serious war crimes breaches to the ICC and that it would have the same investigatory and prosecutorial powers as Arbour's office now possesses. But any member of the Security Council can also block prosecution or prevent referrals of their nationals to the permanent court. These clauses in the draft statute leave Arbour deeply sceptical about the future of the ICC, which in any event is unlikely to see the light of day for several years at least.[1] Far from thinking of her own experience at the Hague as belonging to a rising tide of international interventions, trumping state sovereignty, she fears that it will have turned out to be the high-water mark, and that once she leaves, once the Tribunal finishes its work, the tide will ebb and state sovereignty will re-assert itself. Whatever high-minded aspirations she brought to the job when she arrived three years ago are now tempered with scepticism.

The moral universalism Arbour is charged to enforce – the idea that war crimes in a small village in south-eastern Europe are our business as much as theirs – turns out to be a lot less universal than she supposed when she took the job. In the Rwanda tribunal she secured the first conviction for genocide since the Genocide Convention was created in 1948, and the first admission of guilt by a sitting head of state, Jean Kambanda, for his part in orchestrating the murder of Rwanda's Tutsi population between April and June 1994. 'Kambanda pleading guilty is like Milosevic pleading guilty. Kambanda admitted his culpability in the genocide of 800,000 people. Can you imagine that happening in Europe? It's massive.' But she ruefully observes: 'You can't get anybody interested.' Here again, she has learned a lot about the predictable partialities of the Western moral imagination – zeroing in on Kosovo, ignoring Rwanda, leaving everyone outside the North Atlantic world to wonder whether this moral universalism she is charged to enforce is just another song the West sings in praise of itself.

So her years at the Tribunal have been Louise Arbour's moral education – and they are now coming to an end. She's bought a house in Ottawa and in mid-September she takes up her seat on the Canadian Supreme Court. I ask her whether the Supreme Court job was a train she simply had to catch. 'No, this job was the train I had to leave.' The answer deftly sidesteps the question of whether the chance to take a seat on the Court and cap her professional career in Canada played a role in the timing of the Milosevic indictment.

No, that's not how it was. The real story of her resignation, she insists, was that she was reaching the end of her effective-ness as a prosecutor. To explain why, she lifts the curtain on her real life, the real story, just a fraction, and you see what it must have been like in those meetings trying to get the intelligence co-operation necessary for the Milosevic indictment: 'I beg all the time. Money, political support. So I have to beg, praise, sing, threaten, but I have nothing to give in return. It comes to a point where somebody has to come to this fresh. There are certain things you can't do twice. You can paint someone into a corner once. After that, they'll crush you.' She makes an eloquent bug-squashing gesture with two fingers.

The gesture is more amused than resentful: as if she actually relishes how political, how devious the high-minded world of international criminal prosecution actually turned out to be. What you glimpse here is that there is politics in everything, especially in justice, and lots of hypocrisy too, and that to be a successful prosecutor you have to be an adroit exploiter of the hypocrisy of the powerful: making presidents and prime ministers, foreign ministers and intelligence chiefs feel the price

of not actually practicing what they preach. You do that by threatening and you do that by getting results they don't necessarily want.

And so I ask her whether she will miss it. 'Of course. How could I not? So much I'd like to do. I'm not worried that it's fragile or going to fall to pieces or that I'm indispensable. It's got this huge momentum.' But then she pauses and added: 'The hard part will be not being part of it.' For an instant this brisk, cheerful woman's face is traversed by melancholy.

In the village of Celine, Bill Gent's team has finished their work in the ravine. Their report is already in their laptops. It will establish the identities of those who died; what bullets, what caliber and at what range (very close) the killing was done. It isn't forensic's business to establish who was to blame. But the villagers themselves probably know better than Bill Gent or Louise Arbour who pulled the triggers. There was the Serb neighbor who daubed 'Klinton-Hitler' on the green metal gate to his courtyard in the village; there were the men in ski-masks who came from the next village. Everyone knows who they were.

The day after Arbour's visit to Celine a thickset man in a T-shirt with a dark beard line handed me a packet which at first I took to be his holiday snaps. Fifty glossy pictures: bodies, bodies, bodies. In my hands it felt like pornography and I handed it back. In his hands, it is documentation: how his uncle and aunt, cousins and sister looked when the work of killing was done.

When you see the pictures, it becomes obvious that in Kosovo justice is in a race with revenge, and revenge is likely to win. Revenge is so much faster. The villagers know this and

Louise Arbour knows this. She knows that her tribunal is unlikely ever to find, let alone punish the individuals who killed the villagers of Celine. Many of the killers left in June, on the tops of the Serbian tanks, jeering at the Western press, safe in the knowledge that they were heading northward to a life of impunity.

So what exactly can she do for the villagers of Celine and for the scores of villages of Kosovo where mass graves have been found? Indicting Milosevic is not nothing, collecting the stories – as her investigators have done – is not nothing. Establishing the bare bones of truth – as Bill Gent's team has done – is not nothing. But finally it is insufficient. There is no response adequate to what you encounter when you finally make the journey up the ravine behind the village of Celine.

Five villagers had been caught in the yard of one of the farms, and when they tried to hide in a car, the car was set on fire. Five people died right there, and when it was over, the men who did it tipped the blackened shell on top of the bodies to hide them. When this was going on, the women and children from the village houses nearby must have decided to flee up the ravine. You can see the mattresses that they threw out of their windows to catch their fall or their children's fall. There is a hat box by the side of the track near one house, and a shiny brown wig has fallen out of it on to the grass. Up the narrow green funnel of a track behind the house you go, past the rotting cow, past the clothes and shoes, muddy and wet, abandoned by the path in the panic of flight, not a military uniform in sight, just domestic intimacy in horror strewn about a dark ravine, until you reach the top, just at the point where the trees break and the steeply sloping wheat fields lay. That was where they were cornered, where the men who had come by the upper road met

them and cut off their last escape to the woods. That is where they were cut down, at close range. I have seen the pictures. I do not want to describe them. I will only say that there were twenty-one people, all but three of them women and children. Their bodies have been removed for burial by the village and so all you see at the top of the ravine is a shallow grave, eighteen inches deep, ten feet wide, six feet across. And strewn nearby sodden mud-smeared mattresses, blankets, pyjama tops, under-wear and a child's button-up white sandal. And through the dark tunnel of the ravine, stretching back to the village, the dense, sweet, overpowering odour of death.

It will be a strange afterlife for Louise Arbour, as a robed judge in the Supreme Court of a peaceable kingdom, a long way away from ravines where children were murdered. Already she tells herself not to feel guilty for leaving, for stopping now.

She leaves behind painful expectations. These encompass more than justice, and in any event, I do not think the villagers expect justice. They will have to be satisfied with revenge – and already the sound of gunfire and the smell of Serbian houses going up in smoke is affording such satisfaction as revenge ever provides. But beyond revenge, the villagers seem to want recognition and acknowledgment. Otherwise suffering is just suffering: pointless, stupid, ruinous. What they expected from Louise Arbour, what they stood for hours in the sun awaiting was recognition. That someone important would pay attention to their reality and say that this tiny place had not been for-gotten. The recognition she can provide, however, is limited. The forensic report into the killings in the ravine may be all the recognition Celine ever gets, but the laconic details about ballistic trajectories does at least save facts from the betrayals of

memory in a heartless part of the world where a massacre is no sooner committed than denied. The villagers know that in some imperishable archive, far away in a quiet Dutch city, the story of the ravine will be preserved forever. It will not be enough. Nothing is: I do not suppose the villagers think it is. I do not suppose Louise Arbour thinks it is enough. But it is something.

July 1999

ENEMIES AND FRIENDS

Aleksa Djilas.
'Windows '99', postcard on sale in the streets of Belgrade.
Michael Ignatieff at Stankovec.

Enemies and Friends

In the total wars of the twentieth century, when battle began, communication between enemies ceased. Enemy nationals were expelled or thrown into internment camps. The postal service stopped carrying messages from the other side. Friendships ruptured. In place of contact, vituperation. Instead of communication, propaganda.

In virtual war the telephone lines stay open. You talk to your enemy as you fight him. General Wesley Clark spoke to the Yugoslav Chief of Staff at least once during the campaign, warning him that if he sent any of his navy out into the Adriatic, it would be sunk. Contact wasn't restricted to the generals. From any European or North American city, you could phone Belgrade and hear the shells of your own air forces landing on the city of your friends.

A strange and often painful dialogue across battle-lines then ensued. Throughout the bombing, the wife of a senior official in the American State Department remained in contact with her friends in Belgrade by e-mail. When CNN carried pictures of the crowds massing on the Belgrade bridges, carrying candles and wearing target signs, her electronic messages warned her friends: 'Stay off the bridges!'

This contact reduced the moral estrangement between the two sides. It seemed ridiculous, for example, to think of my Serbian friends as enemies, though that was what they were in formal terms. Each side did attempt to demonize the other – as in the good old days of wars past – but there was an element of half-heartedness and insincerity about it. The Serbian regime made feeble play with equivalence between Clinton and Hitler, and tried to make an association between the bombing of Belgrade in 1999 and the bombing of the city by the Germans in 1941. Our side's propaganda was just as equivocal. NATO's leaders maintained that 'our quarrel is not with the Serbian people.' This did not prevent all atrocities from being attributed, willy nilly, to 'the Serbs' but this propaganda too lacked real conviction. Only wars of national survival turn into wars between peoples, with the mutual demonization which follows. Our leaders presented the contest as a moral struggle but the public did not seem to respond. They did not clamor for images of our 'evil' enemy in order to confirm their convictions, because the convictions were not particularly strong to begin with.

The NATO side stopped short of total caricature, not because of any very great tenderness towards the Serbian people, but simply because channels with the other side remained open throughout the war. Journalists reported what it was like for an ordinary Serbian family to be bombed. Thanks to television, we saw the stunned survivors of our own bombs and that made it more difficult to conserve a state of righteous abstraction towards what they were going through. E-mails, faxes and phone-calls all continued to flow across the battle-lines. The intelligence services of both sides monitored the traffic, but they did not stop it. It was too useful. The Serbs thought – rightly – that it would make us both more hesitant or more discriminate. NATO thought communication with our side might weaken their morale. It did not.

This state of relative transparency made it possible for both sides to anticipate each other's next move. In Belgrade, everyone who had satellite TV watched CNN and Sky News for the NATO briefings, looking for hints of upcoming targets. For days before downtown Belgrade was struck, e-mails and phone messages flew between the Serb capital and the West, as friends, now virtual enemies, exchanged rumors about upcoming strikes.

The transparency of virtual war had direct military consequences. The demonstrations on the Belgrade bridges in late March and early April were more effective in protecting these bridges than the Serb anti-aircraft defenses. Those circular targets – worn by the demonstrators – showed up well on television and they were designed to make NATO stay its hand. What the targets actually meant was: we are blameless objects of your wrath, innocent victims of your weaponry. A feeling of injured innocence, of being misunderstood by the whole world, helped sustain Serb morale to the last days of the war.

I was in Hungary when the bombing began on March 24 and immediately phoned my friend Aleksa Djilas – a writer, historian, son of Milovan Djilas, former Yugoslavia's most famous dissident – at his apartment in downtown Belgrade,

Palmoticeva 8. The lady who looks after the kids went to get him, and while I waited for him to come to the phone I could hear a knife chopping vegetables on a kitchen counter and children chattering around a table waiting for their dinner to be served. When Aleksa picked up the phone, almost his first words were: 'I understand the mechanism of madness on my side. But do you understand the mechanism of madness on yours?'[1] I said it wasn't madness. It was the only alternative. He disagreed. The atmosphere was chilly, but we kept talking. Some mutual need – to explain, to justify – kept us talking throughout the war.

When I phoned in early April, I could hear the rat-a-tat-tat of anti-aircraft fire in the background. Aleksa asked me whether the rumor was true that the bombing of the Defense Ministry was imminent. I said I'd heard the same rumor. He told me to tell my NATO contacts that there was no one in the building except pension and payroll clerks. All the military command staff were in bunkers. I told him I would relay the message and did – as if NATO targeteers didn't know it already.

As the bombing of Belgrade intensified, wealthy Belgrade citizens went south to Greece or north to Hungary. Those with country cousins evacuated their families to small towns and villages. Aleksa and his wife, Oligica (pronounced Olgitsa), and their two children stayed put in Palmoticeva. The bombing began usually under cover of darkness and the state of alert lasted as long as ten hours at a time. Sleep was driven forward into the late watches of the night. The family stayed up till two or three in the morning, lying down in their clothes as the authorities recommended. They stayed away from the neighborhood air-raid shelters because the atmosphere of close confinement frightened the children. Back in the apartment, the sky would light up with fireworks, and they would keep away from the windows which shook with the reverberations of the distant explosions. When I phoned Aleksa there were times when I could hear nervous excitement in his voice, as he described the flashes in the sky, but as the bombing went on, excitement was followed by powerlessness and depression.

In late April I phone Aleksa again, and this time from Stankovec refugee camp in Macedonia. I wanted him to see what I was seeing: the refugees from Pristina, lined up five hundred yards long queuing for ready-meals in their yellow packets. I wanted him to hear what they had told me: how their homes and apartments had been marked with crosses; how they had been given five minutes to pack and get out; how they had been robbed and intimidated; how they had been loaded on to railway cars and shunted to the Macedonian border. The grimly efficient organization that went into their expulsion and the dire echoes from times past made a deep impression upon me. I told Aleksa that he might not believe the Western media, and he certainly shouldn't believe his own, but he should believe me: a whole people had been deported and driven from their homes. He listened and he said, in a strained, tight voice, that yes, it was certainly true.

Preposterous as it sounds, that was what I wanted – an admission. I told him I would come see him in Belgrade, but I had to wait until the war was over before I kept my promise.

When I arrived in late July, Belgrade airport was all but deserted. The only flights in or out were to Moscow or Peking. The river Danube which flows through the city was empty of barges and boats. The bridges had been downed upriver at Novi Sad and freight traffic along the waterway had come to a standstill. In the square beside the Hotel Moskva, there were small demonstrations of angry Serbs from Kosovo, demanding shelter and relief. Further down the street, in the pedestrian precinct which leads from Terazije to the Kalemegdan park, the American, German and French cultural centers and the British Council building stood exposed to the street, windows smashed, papers strewn about inside the gutted remains. These islands where Belgrade intellectuals and students used to go to learn foreign languages and read the foreign press had been destroyed by angry crowds on the first night of the NATO bombing.

But the mood of fury had dissipated. McDonald's had also been attacked, but it was back in business, serving hamburgers and Cokes. It had passed seamlessly from being a hated symbol of American imperialism to a longed-for point of contact with Western mass culture. On the streets, newsagents were already selling an extraordinary set of postcards depicting Belgrade by night: the tracery of anti-aircraft fire over the apartment blocks of Novi Belgrade; the flames leaping from the burning headquarters of the Serbian socialist party; the gaping glassfree windows of the Ministry of Defense, with the caption: NATO SOFT, Windows 99.

There weren't many foreigners in town, so these postcards were intended for the people of Belgrade, more of the gallows humor which has become the city's trademark this past decade. The postcards also implied that for most of the people the bombing had been a lurid show, terrifying if you were in the suburbs, near the oil depots and the military bases, but merely dramatic and exciting if you lived in the center. Modern precision bombing does kill, but when it does, it has a peculiar unreality even to its victims. It becomes – like a light show or a fireworks display – the kind of event you commemorate by buying a postcard. In order to grasp 'the lightness of being' implied by these cards, it is worth remembering that no one would have thought of selling postcards of the ruins of Hamburg or Dresden in 1945.

The bombing, needless to say, had also been a light show for the Western TV audiences, and this made it easier to support. Unreality eases moral consent. It's easier to bomb a city – or support its bombardment – if you've never been there, if you can dematerialize the place in your mind and turn it into a target pure and simple.

The bombing of Belgrade was never an abstraction to me. When the bombs landed, they were not hitting an abstract target, dematerialized by moral certainties, but a real place whose streets and parks called up childhood memories of my own. I had vivid memories of the two years I lived there as a child – 1958-1959 – in Tito's heyday when my father was a diplomat and we lived in a big house in the leafy hills of Dedinje, near Tito's official residence, and I rooted for Red Star football club and spoke a language – Serbo-Croatian – which no longer officially exists.

On my arrival in July, I went straight to Palmoticeva 8, the apartment on the leafy street behind the parliament building in central Belgrade where Aleksa lives with Olgica, and his children. He is a tall, trim, good-looking man in his forties, with the high forehead and high hairline of his father, but a gentler face. He is devoted to his wife, a chain-smoking dentist with a long and expressive face and a droll way of looking at him in mock-dismay.

Over the years I have known Aleksa, I have come to see him as a man who keeps self-doubt and melancholy at bay with a stream of jokes and mimicry. He has an especially good ear for the menacing yet hollow rhetoric of Slobodan Milosevic and has even a short collection of the great man's aphorisms:

'The difficulties are neither unexpected nor insurmountable.'

'The difficulties should not be a reason to demobilize, but to mobilize ourselves.'

'The future will be beautiful, and it is not far away.'[2]

Djilas also had an extended repertoire of war jokes. 'What's the fastest route between Belgrade and Pristina? Drive to Albania, take a ferry to Bari, get a train to Aviano. There's a plane leaving for Belgrade every five minutes.'

He was also a connoisseur of ethnic jokes: the Slovenian boy who comes home to tell his parents that he is coming out of the closet and living with a boy called Jovan. How could you do this to us? they cry. Gay is one thing, but living with a *Serb*?

Or this one about the Belgrade boy with a Jewish mother and a Serbian father. 'What's my nationality?' the boy asks. You're Jewish, says his mother. No, you're Serb, says his father. But why do you want to know they both ask him. 'Well, this kid wants to sell me his bicycle. So I'm wondering: should I bargain with him or just steal it?'

Aleksa can see that these jokes make me wince, halfway between laughter and embarrassment. But he keeps at it, both to laugh at my Western political correctness, but also to put ironic distance between himself and the Balkan madhouse he lives in, where even a child is a Jew or a Serb, or a Croat or a Kosovar, before they are anything else.

His flat on Palmoticeva – creaking parquet floors, long

corridors, high ceilings – belonged to his father and mother, and the dark rooms are lined with his father's books, pictures and photographs. Aleksa's father Milovan was an extraordinary man: born on a farm in the mountains of Montenegro, he came north to Belgrade in the 1930s and became a Communist student, serving a prison term for anti-government agitation under the royalist dictatorship. With Josip Broz Tito, he founded the Communist Partisan movement which led the Yugoslav Communist Revolution. Between 1941 and 1944, Djilas himself was in the thick of the fighting against the German invaders and against the royalist anti-Communist partisans, known as the Chetniks. In 1944, Djilas was dispatched to Moscow to negotiate aid for the Communist Partisans from the Soviets, and there he had the first of three meetings with Stalin. Djilas senior was a powerful writer and his portrait of Stalin – published in 1962 as *Conversations with Stalin* – is the most intimate glimpse we have of the monster in the flesh, small, flabby, exhausted and irritable, with black and irregular teeth and 'watchful, wary, yellow eyes.' Djilas had come to worship, but he came away from the Soviet Union appalled and disillusioned.

Yugoslavia's break with the Soviet Union in 1948 – the first attempt by an Eastern European Communist state to define its own national path to socialism – would not have happened without Djilas. And it was Djilas who tried to define this 'national' path, the Yugoslav experiment with workers' control. But by 1953, whilst he was at the pinnacle of power, he realized that the 'new class' – the new Communist elite – was making it impossible to democratize socialism. After publishing outspoken attacks on the privileges of the party elite, he broke with Tito – the first Eastern European party leader to become a dissident – and spent nine hard years in Tito's jails, emerging only in 1967. He returned to the apartment at Palmoticeva, a stone's throw away from the Central Committee headquarters where he had once ruled the country, and lived there until his death in 1995, too distinguished and courageous to be touched, watching – with deepening gloom – the slow disintegration of the country he and Tito had founded.[3]

I met Milovan Djilas once, in the apartment in Palmoticeva in the spring of 1993. He was a compact old man with white hair, alert, austere, guarded and highly intelligent. He wore faded corduroys, and his bearing was stooped. Stefica, his beloved wife for forty years, was already dying and though he never referred to it, he was clearly struggling with the prospect of losing her. As we talked, Bosnian Serb paramilitaries were laying siege to Sarajevo and the nation he had helped to found was being torn apart by ethnic war. I asked him why his country had been destroyed, and he replied that Tito had failed to allow democracy in Yugoslavia. He had turned out to be 'both the master and the slave of the privileged class.' He said this with the gloomy relish of a man who had lived long enough to see his prophecies come true. His last words of warning to me were: 'Don't demonize the Serbs.'

Aleksa was born in 1953 – on the eve of his father's fall from power – and grew up visiting his father in prison. He remembered the time he and his mother were waiting in front of the prison in Sremska Mitrovica, north of Belgrade, and he began playing with a Roma – a gypsy child – who was waiting with his mother to visit his father, serving a sentence for theft. Why is your father in prison, the gypsy boy asked.

'Because of a book.'

'You mean he stole a book?'

'No, he wrote one.'

'But that's impossible. No one goes to jail for writing a book.'

With time, it became a matter of pride and honor to have a father who had gone to jail for writing a book. But in the 1950s – when the Hungarian revolution had been smashed, when there was not a single chink of light in the Soviet system – it must have seemed a lonely, even desperate destiny. But his father was made of very stubborn Montenegrin material. Aleksa remembered asking his father, late in life, whether it had all been worth it – the dissent, the disgrace, the years in prison – and his father replied that his only regret was that he had not done it earlier. When Aleksa tells you this, his face lights up at the memory.

Aleksa spent nearly eleven years outside Yugoslavia, first at the London School of Economics and then at Harvard, writing a book on the role of the Communist party – and his father – in creating the ideology and practice of 'brotherhood and unity' which held Yugoslavia together until Tito's death.[4] During his time abroad, he edited a Serbian-language anthology of human rights and English translations of the Belgrade dissidents. Anti-party articles in the émigré Yugoslav press earned him official denunciation as a counter-revolutionary agent. When his passport expired in 1983, he applied for and received political asylum in Britain.

He could have stayed in the West but his parents were getting old – and he wanted to be with them. Besides, he says, 'the worse it got in my country, the more I wanted to return.' When I call this typical Serbian masochism, he laughs and then shakes his head. It was proving embarrassing to be sitting at Harvard commenting on your own country, as if you were a foreigner. So he returned to the apartment in Palmoticeva, and to a post Cold War version of his father's life as a distinguished, and so far untouchable dissident in Milosevic's Serbia. He has become the acceptable face of the Serbian intelligentsia, flying off to Athens or Amsterdam, Boston or New York, to lecture or take part in panels on matters Balkan. Back home he occupies an ambiguous position: because he defends his country, he has forfeited many of his Western friendships, but because he despises both government and opposition at home, he has no political role or base. He is marooned among the dwindling band of independent thinkers who have not been corrupted or forced into exile by the regime. Western liberals want him to disavow his country and his people; he refuses, and so the whisper goes out that he has 'gone nationalist,' when the reality is more complex. He is a patriot of a country – Yugoslavia – which no longer exists; an internal exile in a state ruined by a clique he despises; a paid-up member of the Western European intellectual club, which unfortunately no longer accepts membership from Serbs.

We spent a long day together, visiting the ruins left behind by NATO's air-strikes. The first was the Serbian TV center, a five-minute walk from his apartment. When Aleksa got there, about an hour after the strike on April 17, it was three o'clock in the morning, and bloodied, dust-covered survivors were wandering around in shock whilst rescue teams were frantically trying to dig bodies out of the ruins. Now, grass was beginning to grow at the base of the ruined studio block. On the glass entrance door of the untouched administrative block, the death notices of the fifteen victims were beginning to peel away. He wanted me to notice one in particular, a female make-up artist in her twenties. She had been engaged to be married. So they buried her, he said, in a white coffin.

I had seen the footage. Reality is always otherwise. The destruction was awesome because it was so unbelievably precise: not the administration block next door, not the still intact studios under blue reflecting glass on the other side, but just this one single studio area, methodically crushed, as if a hand from the sky had pushed down floor by floor, seizing hold of human beings, chairs, tables, equipment, monitors and plunging them into the pile of debris at the bottom.

Faced with the impact, I tried to remember the justifications: the need to annihilate the propaganda heart of the regime, the dual-use of TV transmitters as military relays, etc. To which Aleksa replied, 'There was a lot of propaganda, but it was not the kind many people imagined. You didn't have television programs inciting people to commit acts of violence against Albanians.' I was tempted to reply – but didn't – that they didn't need to incite anyone. The deeds were already underway: the uniformed marauders were already going from house to house. And what about television reporting of the ethnic cleansing? Were Serbs ever told the truth? I wanted to know.

'Well, let's say the plight of the refugees was under reported,' Aleksa conceded. Meaning, I say, that their plight wasn't reported at all. 'It's a serious sin of omission but you know, do you kill so many people because of them? And what about NATO propaganda? In any case, killing people who work in the media is totally unacceptable under any circumstances.'

We resumed our walk past the church where he and his wife were married, through a park and down the Kneza Milosa – the straight, tree-lined avenue which leads into the center of town. We passed the Canadian embassy on one side, and the American on the other, both now daubed with graffiti and their windows smashed. We stopped in front of the Defense Ministry, a modern red-stone complex built in Tito's heyday to house what was then the headquarters of one of the largest armed forces in the world. B-2 strikes had reduced parts of it to mangled structural steel and pulverized concrete and left the rest windowless and abandoned, as empty and eerie as they must have been on the night they were attacked.

One of the guilty secrets about bombed ruins is that they are beautiful. The destruction here – as if some giant had clawed his hand across five hundred yards of windows and pulled them each from their frames – was astonishing. The destruction was also a puzzle, because NATO knew that there would be no one in the building. The nerve centers of the regime were underground in bunkers in army bases on the outskirts of town. These too were hit, but since they had been constructed to survive nuclear attack, the strikes were more in the nature of a message – we know where you are – rather than a serious attempt at degrading their command and control.

So why bother to hit empty buildings? Aleksa believed that the real object of the strikes was civilian morale: 'It was vandalism whose main purpose was to intimidate the population.' They were hoping Serbs would turn against Milosevic once the sacrifices became too great but they had to do it in such a way that Western public opinion would accept it. And they did accept it. Where were the demonstrations in European and American cities against the bombing? The reality, he insisted, was that if our pilots had been downed, or our ships sunk, our so-called moral restraint would have disappeared in an instant. We weren't even prepared to risk our own soldiers in battle. 'They were ready to risk the life of my wife and my children but not their soldiers' lives.' If we had really fought them, face to face, he was implying, and if we had faced death, as they had done, then we might have had his respect. There was real bitterness in his voice, at the hypocrisy of our willingness to kill in the name of our values, but not to die.

We walked along Kneza Milosa to the police headquarters at the top of the street. These intimidating four-story buildings, once home to Tito's UDBA, the secret police that had arrested and interrogated Aleksa's father, now served as the head-quarters of the units that had spearheaded the ethnic cleansing in Kosovo. Knowing this, I took cold satisfaction from the destruction, the curtains flapping through empty window frames, the glass still unswept on the street below, the policemen's lockers tumbled about, the interrogation cells in the basement now scarred with flames. The 'MUP' – as the hated police were known – was as legitimate a target as there ever could be in a war like this. Feeling the need to win some ground back, I told Aleksa so. He listened in silence.

Then I asked him what he would have done if he had been drafted. 'I would not try to avoid being drafted because I think we were unjustly attacked. I would have had no moral problems fighting against NATO. We had a right and a duty to defend our country.'

Having made this solemn pronouncement, he pulled back, looking for a joke to break the silence which followed. He remembered that when they were being bombed, he and his friends used to fantasize about what would happen if Serbia actually defeated NATO and won. They dreamed of dividing the world. 'Typical Serbian grandiosity, right?' His friend Borka would get Spain, and another friend wanted both Switzerland and Portugal. 'But that's not right, is it?' I agreed that it was greedy.

As we walked back to his apartment I brought up the Racak massacre of January 15, when forty-five Kosovar civilians were found slaughtered. He denied that it was a massacre as such, rather a shoot-out with the KLA guerillas in which civilians may have been gunned down as well. He insisted that there was no ethnic cleansing as such before the bombing began, just people driven up into the hills to escape the war between Serbs and the KLA. The most he would accept was that Serb forces used 'excessive force' – but they were faced with a terrorist threat, and their policemen, soldiers and postmen were being murdered daily. 'To attack with one thousand bombers a sovereign country in Europe not threatening anyone against the whole line of international treaties and agreements is completely outrageous.' NATO may portray the Serbs as a pariah nation, he wanted me to know, but most of Latin America, most of Africa and Asia – 'several billion people in fact' – had been against the NATO strikes. How he knew this he did not say, but the point was to strip away my pretensions to universality, to make me feel a guilty party to good old-fashioned Western imperialism.

But did he really consider the Serb regime guiltless? Was NATO to blame for the ethnic cleansing? No, he conceded, only for making a bad situation worse.

And then he asked me whether I knew which country in Europe had the largest refugee population. 'Serbia,' I replied, knowing where we were headed. He pressed on: if you in the West were so concerned about ethnic cleansing, why did you do nothing to stop the Croats in the summer of 1995 when they drove 250,000 Serbs out of Croatia? And why have you done nothing to stop the expulsion of Serbs from Kosovo?

'Do you want me say that's a crime? Yes, I think that's a crime.'

He was in his stride now. Soon Kosovo would become independent and the Serbs – who had been there since the sixth century AD would never return. Their monasteries and convents would be torn down. The grass would grow over their graves. What had the West accomplished? It had promised to defend a multi-ethnic Kosovo and all it had achieved was the ethnic cleansing of the Serbs. And the Roma, the gypsies too. It won't be multi-ethnic, your Kosovo, he told me, and I doubt that it will be democratic.

We walked past more rubble, through the back streets behind the parliament building, the district of the city Aleksa thinks of as his village, and his argument widened out. You Western liberals, he said, don't understand anything about nationalism. You think ethnic cleansing is a Balkan invention. But look at the history of Western Europe. All modern nations are formed in blood, by the eviction of religious and ethnic minorities. All attempts to stop the formation of ethnically homogeneous national states have failed. Ethnic homogeneity is the core of national cohesion. The Turks drove out the Greeks; the Lithuanians drove out the Poles; the Poles and the Czechs drove out the ethnic Germans; and everybody drove out the Jews. When nationalism allies itself to democracy, the result is the mono-ethnic nation state.

He had said as much in an article in 1995:

The civil war in Yugoslavia is part of the same process of border formation and ethnic homogenization which the rest of Europe has already been through. What is happening is not Balkanization but Europeanization, and it is irreversible.[5]

To say this was to assert that ethnic cleansing was built into all of our histories, that it was Western Europe's dirty little secret. I protested that he was playing a game of moral equivalencies. If everyone is guilty, no one is. He said he didn't approve of the history; he merely thought it was unavoidable.

What became clear to me – afterwards, not at the time – was that Eastern and Western Europe had lived different histories which each side comprehensively misunderstood. Just as the former Yugoslavia entered its dire experiment in state formation through ethnic cleansing, Western European and North American societies began to see themselves as multi-ethnic societies. Just as Serbia embraced the ideology of Greater Serbia, we embraced 'difference,' 'tolerance' and the whole moral paraphernalia of multi-ethnic self-congratulation. All of this sustained, of course, by the memory of the Holocaust, and by that refrain, Never Again.

To be sure, this embrace of multi-ethnicity was false at any number of levels: from immigration controls to de facto residential segregation, Western societies have not practiced what they preach. They remain overwhelmingly white and they continue to distribute power and influence unequally. But they *imagine* themselves as communities of difference, and when their leaders try to define what these societies 'stand for,' the embrace of difference – however problematic and even empty this idea may seem – is at the heart of whatever collective project remains for us. This self-image – not the reality, but the virtual moral image – was what held the West together in its stand against Serbian ethnic cleansing. And it was this self-approving moral image which seemed so false to the Serbs. Who were *we* to tell them how to live with their minorities? Who were we to preach tolerance? And who were we to bomb them when their leaders refused to capitulate?

The only honest answer to these arguments is that they are an example of moral perfectionism. The requirement that 'he who casts the first stone should be without sin' is a guarantee of inaction. The fact that the West does not live up to its ideals does not invalidate the ideals or invalidate their defense. Ideals are frequently defended by people with dirty hands – and bad consciences. That is what our argument came down to – bad consciences on both sides.

The bad conscience on my side was that we had talked the language of ultimate causes and practiced the art of minimum risk. Aleksa's bad conscience was that he had lived inside a morally squalid state and had done so little to bring it to its senses. He pleaded that he had given 'dozens of interviews' against the repression of the Albanians: that he had never supported Milosevic's campaign to hold on to Kosovo by terror. Of course it was true, but it did nothing to lift the weight. I had said to him in passing – lest he think my moralizing was leading that way – that I didn't believe in collective guilt. He shot back: 'But I do.'

On my last night in Belgrade, Aleksa invited friends over – fluent English speakers, all of them, with memories of a year at Stanford, or a degree at the Sorbonne, able to commiserate about the rigors of Michigan winters, because they had been at graduate school in Ann Arbor, and so on. It was a mournful evening: I would be leaving the next day. They would be staying. It's still not impossible for them to get exit visas or the hard currency to travel, but it's more and more difficult. Their isolation deepens and it felt palpable in the room.

One of them, Borka Pavicevic, had joined Aleksa and myself in June 1996 when we had flown into Sarajevo, in the first summer after the war in Bosnia. We had gone there for a conference of the European Mozart Foundation in the service of a particularly quixotic liberal illusion: dialogue between enemies after the bitter siege of the city. We met Bosnian Muslims, human rights activists, the exhausted and disillusioned defenders of the old multi-ethnic Sarajevo, whom the Bosnian Serbs on the hillsides above the city had pounded for three horrible years. Borka and Aleksa were among the first Serbs from Belgrade to visit the city, and they ventured out gingerly, careful to speak English rather than Serbian on the streets, so as not to attract attention, looking mournfully at the pitted and scarred monuments to the ugly determination of the Serbian gunners. During that visit, we had meetings – Croats, Muslims, Serbs – around a table in a partially bombed hotel. They were cold, clenched meetings which were supposed to explore the possibility of whether one day former enemies could ever write a common history of the catastrophe they had all suffered. Borka and Aleksa said little and left the talking to the victims, the thin, tired Bosnian Muslims. No, the Bosnians said finally. A common history is not possible. We cannot even agree on the facts. And agreeing about who is to blame – and that is what matters – will never happen. They did not even look at Aleksa and Borka.

Borka and I recalled that visit to Sarajevo together. She is a fiery and unstoppable talker, with a husky, smoke-filled rasp to her voice, and the mocking irony of the Belgrade intellectual class, the kind of irony that leads her to run, year after year, a Center for Cultural Decontamination, a theater, lecture hall and art gallery, where Belgraders can come to escape the maddening ideological noise of Milosevic's media. I asked her how she felt when the bombing started. A certain elation, she conceded. When I asked her why, she said: 'I felt de-Nazified.'

Others laughed and agreed, Aleksa included. They knew – because they had read *The New Republic* and *The Wall Street Journal* – that Westerners kept asking why not even so-called 'liberal' intellectuals in Belgrade had questioned Milosevic's repression of the Kosovars, why there had been no demonstrations, no protests against the butchery in Srebrenica, the massacre at Racak. Well, now the years of guilt by association could be thrown off. The shame could be passed around. The bombing had turned them into victims too – and victims by definition must be innocent.

Still Borka and Aleksa and the others in that room were too smart to take refuge for long in fables of innocence and the strategies of exculpation. Yet they were trapped between shame at their own country and fury at the blithe moral certainties of their erstwhile Western friends. Between these poles, they chose to live in the valiant, but forlorn world of jokes.

I wanted to say – as we sat in a circle in a dark apartment on a summer's night – that I did not believe in collective guilt, not theirs, not ours. It seemed – though I could not say this either – that we were not actually talking about guilt at all, just radical disagreement, beyond argument or resolution. The question was whether friendships can overcome politics: and what price friendship between enemies exacts in the long term. I said none of this, of course. I just raised my glass and said, 'To my Serbian friends.' To which, Aleksa replied, after a pause, 'Your Yugoslav friends.' And that was where we ended – united at least in common sorrow for a country which no longer existed.

July 1999

VIRTUAL WAR

The USS *Phillipine Sea* launches a Cruise missile at targets in
Kosovo, March 24, 1999.
(AP Photo/US Navy, Renso Amariz)

V i r t u a l   W a r

1. *Moral Impunity*

The Kosovo campaign achieved its objectives without a single NATO combat fatality. From a military standpoint, this is an unprecedented achievement. From an ethical standpoint, it transforms the expectations that govern the morality of war. The tacit contract of combat throughout the ages has always assumed a basic equality of moral risk: kill or be killed. Accordingly violence in war avails itself of the legitimacy of self-defense. But this contract is void when one side begins killing with impunity. Put another way, a war ceases to be just when it becomes a turkey shoot. While our opponent in Kosovo was not prostrated – Serb air defenses continued firing until the last day of the air-campaign – the contest was so unequal that NATO could only preserve its sense of moral advantage by observing especially strict rules of engagement.

NATO presented these rules – which tried to limit civilian casualties – as a sign of moral superiority. But one could argue that their real purpose was to assuage NATO's unease about its own impunity. Had its military personnel faced risks equal to those run by its opponent, it would have responded robustly, even savagely. If one of its ships had been sunk or had it lost substantial numbers of pilots, it might well have become more punitive and less discriminating in its use of air power. Military superiority, rather than conscience alone, dictated restraint. Where risk is not shared equally with an opponent, damage must be minimized.

The Yale legal philosopher, Paul Kahn, has argued that 'riskless warfare in pursuit of human rights' is a moral contradiction. The concept of human rights assumes that all human life is of equal value. Risk-free warfare presumes that our lives matter more than those we are intervening to save.[1] Does this mean then that we have to lay down our lives in order to prove our moral seriousness? Does war only become legitimate when the carnage is equal on both sides? Surely not. Interventions which minimize casualties to both sides must be the better strategy. Evidently, there is no virtue in risk for the sake of risk, and no commander worth his stars will do anything other than seek victory with minimum loss to his own troops. The real question is whether risk-free warfare can work.

Western interventions in the post-Cold War era have struggled to achieve their ends at the lowest possible military cost. Because the Kosovo campaign obtained its objectives without sacrificing a single Allied life, it appears to vindicate the strategy and tactics of virtual war. It also appears to vindicate the right of humanitarian intervention, and the exercise of this right has become the chief remaining *raison d'etre* for the armed forces of Western states.[2] The 'right' of these forces to intervene is vigorously contested both by the Soviet Union and China as well as by many non-aligned states in the Third World, and it has no status in customary or statutory international law. It prevails simply because the West has the power to enforce its writ.

The fact that this new resort to military force is justified in humanitarian terms should give us pause, especially when the force can be exercised with lethal precision. For here we have an ancient specter in modern form: violence which moralizes itself as justice and which is unrestrained by consequences.

We need to consider the implications of this new form of military violence, especially in relation to the issue of democratic control. If violence ceases to be fully real to the citizens in whose name it is exercised will they continue to restrain the executive resort to precision lethality? This becomes an urgent issue in the context of overwhelming American military superiority. If one side of a future conflict is shielded from the reality of war and its consequences, why should it continue to be guided by restraint?

Fortunately – at least for those who advocate caution in the use of military force – modern democratic elites are increasingly reluctant to go to war. Precision violence is now at the disposal of a risk-adverse culture, unconvinced by the language of military sacrifice, skeptical about the costs of foreign adventures and determined to keep out of harm's way.

The Kosovo operation is the paradigm of this paradoxical form of warfare: where technological omnipotence is vested in the hands of risk-adverse political cultures. In order to explore where this kind of war is leading us, we need to understand the revolution in military affairs which made it possible and explain why America currently enjoys the monopoly on the new technology. Finally, since no monopoly is ever stable or enduring, we need to ask how other nations will react, and whether the result will be a safer or more dangerous world.

2. The Revolution in Military Affairs

The technologies put to use in Kosovo are the result of a revolution in military affairs – often referred to simply as the RMA – which began in the 1970s and whose purpose was to return war in the West to its position as the continuation of politics by other means. In the 1970s and 1980s, the two super-powers confronted each other with nuclear weapons they could not use and prepared for a war – across the north German plain – which they could not fight. Competition to add to nuclear arsenals was no longer delivering any discernible strategic or political advantage to either side. The only way to get ahead in a nuclear stalemate lay in developing *conventional* weapons that the other side did not possess. The beauty of such weapons was that, unlike the nuclear arsenal, they could be used.

But only in a certain way. To make the use of these weapons politically and morally acceptable, it was essential to increase the precision of their targeting; to minimize the collateral or unintended consequences of their use; and to reduce, if not eliminate, the risk to those who fired them, by keeping them as far away from the battle-line as was consistent with accuracy. From the beginning, therefore, technology was in search of impunity. War that could actually be fought had to be as bloodless, risk-free and precise as possible.

These cultural constraints are not in themselves new. In all previous revolutions in military technology, proponents of new weaponry have overcome moral resistance to their diffusion by arguing that greater precision and lethality would make wars less bloody. In 1621, for instance, the poet John Donne surmised that the recent invention of long-range artillery would bring 'wars to a quicker end than heretofore.' 'A great expense of blood' would be avoided, he claimed, because artillery was both more lethal and more precise than the sword.[3] And the utopia of victory with impunity is also not new. The most perennially popular military manual – Sun Tzu's *The Art of War* – proclaimed almost 2500 years ago that 'to subdue the enemy without fighting is the supreme excellence.'[4]

What was new – as Lawrence Freedman has argued – was the particular political and strategic context in which the new technology made its appearance in the 1970s. Two super-powers each possessed nuclear arsenals which canceled out the other, but which also made them invulnerable to attack. Hence war – at least for them – had become unusable as an instrument of policy. This stalemate could not endure, however. The capacity to wage war after all, is what gives power to nations. One or the other was bound to seek escape from the impasse. Only one of them, however, had the technological capacity to make the break-through.

The dawn of the new age of precision weaponry can be dated to the US Air Force's destruction of the Thanwa Bridge in Vietnam in 1972.[5] The bridge was used to funnel Chinese and Soviet equipment from North to South Vietnam. Unable to take it out with manned aircraft, the Air Force improvised a missile which could be fired from an aircraft and then guided to its target by a technician viewing images of the target beamed back from a television camera attached to the nose of the missile. This attack succeeded, too late to alter the course of the Vietnam War, but it heralded the arrival of a new age of precision weaponry.

Within ten years, the Americans had developed a small arsenal of these precision weapons, using lasers, computers and gun cameras to guide them to their targets. The best known of these was the Cruise missile, an accurate, unmanned system which could be fired from ships or planes at ever-increasing distances from its target.

Of course, this revolution in military affairs was not the result of a single technological breakthrough, but of many in combination: lasers to improve guidance and targeting, computers linked to satellite positioning systems which made pinpoint accuracy possible; propulsion systems which increased the range of conventional rockets, refinements in explosives technology which reduced damage to civilians, as well as unmanned and robotized surveillance drones which eliminated risks to aviators. As a result, America emerged from the 1980s with a technological capability it could actually use.[6] Rogue states like Iraq and Yugoslavia, and weak, failed states like Sudan and Somalia were custom-made as firing ranges for the new technology: they were too weak to resist effectively, and their own behavior was so offensive that they forfeited the support of powerful friends.

Andrew Marshall, the planner most responsible for convincing the Pentagon of the new technology's promise concedes, in his words, that 'the United States was making the revolution, but they (the Russians) were the first to see it in that light.'[7] By the mid 1980s, Russian military thinkers realized what the Americans were doing: making it possible to fight wars again with technologies in which the Russians lagged woefully behind.[8]

Nothing so clearly demonstrated the economic bankruptcy of the whole Communist system as the American lead in the revolution in military affairs. Asked when the doom of the Soviet system was sealed, Mikhail Gorbachev supposedly replied, 'Reykjavik', meaning the summit at which President Reagan presented him with evidence of American superiority in space-based missile defense systems.[9] But Russian alarm about 'Star Wars' was only part of the story: they were also lagging behind in non-nuclear precision weaponry. They could see that a closed society like theirs was unable to compete with an open society, where innovations in computer software – quickly leading to military spin-offs – were coming out of the garages of Californian 20-somethings. America won the Cold War because it entered a new type of economy – based on knowledge and computers – and left its strategic competitor marooned inside the crumbling remains of the industrial era. Even the European countries that also entered the computer era discovered they had been overtaken in the military domain. France, Germany and Britain had rebuilt their economies after the war by allowing the Americans to put up most of the cost of European defense. The distinctive European capitalist model – more focused on social welfare than the Americans – presumed less defense expenditure. In this way, Europeans positioned themselves as economic rivals to the United States in return for accepting their subordination as military powers. Both sides benefited. America gained its unrivaled superiority, and Europe developed its unique system of market capitalism combined with high levels of social welfare spending. The adverse consequences only became apparent in the 1990s when NATO began to police the Balkans. With their miniature versions of World War II armies, the European states lacked the resources to sustain their Balkan contingents. Their boutique armies were incapable of providing more than trip-wire defense of their national territories, and they were only able to combine with American operations in a subordinate role. They were dependent on the Americans for the large aircraft required to lift soldiers into expeditionary battle-zones overseas; and they lacked independent satellite and electronic intelligence capability.

Faced with the widening gulf between themselves and the Americans, the Europeans faced a hard choice: either to subordinate themselves ever further to American military power, or to pool their resources into a joint European capability which while still associated with the US in NATO could also serve as a counter-poise. In December 1999, the European powers committed themselves to the second option: developing a rapid reaction force, under separate command, of up to 60,000 men. Yet their dependence on American precision weaponry remains unaddressed, and the American monopoly on these weapons remains unchallenged.

As early as the Gulf War in 1991, American superiority in precision weapons was plain for all to see. While the number of these weapons used in the air campaign over Iraq was no more than 8 percent of the total ordinance dropped, these weapons – especially the Cruise missile – demonstrated an awesome potential for risk-free lethality.[10] The bombing of Baghdad was the first war as light show and the aerial bombardment of Iraqi forces was the first battle turned into a video-arcade game. The experience transformed public expectation of war. Having been told to prepare for as many as 25,000 casualties, the electorate discovered the intoxicating reality of risk-free warfare.

The full effects of the revolution in precision guidance are only just becoming apparent. Precision guidance can be applied, upward in the chain of destructiveness, to nuclear weapons themselves; and downwards to small arms. Nuclear weapons can be miniaturized: their payloads so reduced and their guidance systems made so precise that they can avoid the indiscriminate destruction which previously made them unusable. Likewise, at the other end of the scale, there is no reason in principle – other than cost – why there cannot be precision guided bullets, computer directed to their targets.

Accuracy at a distance changes the nature and objective of combat. Instead of closing with an opponent, the object is to destroy him at long range, accelerating a long-standing trend: the battlefield has been emptying for centuries.[11] Indeed, striking from a distance makes total force protection a meaningful, if paradoxical goal in modern warfare. Distance also confers political advantages. If you can fight a war from the continental United States, or from a submarine cruising thousands of miles from the target, you are freed from the constraint of securing alliance consent for use of their bases, and from the risk of exposing American assets to attack.

Precision guidance also changes the objective of war. Throughout the industrial era, combatants focused on attrition and destruction: hurling high explosives at the enemy's men and equipment in order to degrade their capacity to continue fighting. Instead of attrition, the aim of post-modern warfare is to strike at the nerve centers – command posts, computer networks – which direct the war-machine. A blinded enemy – without computers, telephones or power – may still have forces capable of attack, but he no longer has the capacity to order them into battle. Command and control can be attacked both by direct missile bombardment and also by information warfare: electronic jamming, release of computer viruses, disinformation and propaganda. Destroying the credibility and reliability of the data on which the enemy bases his decisions becomes just as effective as killing his people or wrecking his cities. In fact it is conceivable to ignore an enemy's fielded forces altogether and concentrate instead on the computers, satellites, radar, telephone systems and power supplies which enable the enemy to make decisions.

The essential choice of the Kosovo war turned on this distinction, with some American air-commanders arguing that the focus of the campaign should be on Serbian command and control in the Belgrade area, while others, like Wesley Clark, believed that the focus should be upon fielded forces, since they were the ones responsible for the massacres and expulsion of the Kosovars. It could be argued that the campaign dragged on for 78 days precisely because NATO failed to make this choice decisively enough. The 'tank-plinking' of the tactical campaign merely drove the Serb military into revetments and dug-outs, while the strategic campaign was never pursued with the ferocity necessary to blind the enemy's command and control.

The Kosovo war demonstrated that strategic campaigns carry their own risks, however. While precision guidance weaponry is supposed to reverse the twentieth-century trend towards ever greater civilian casualties, warfare directed at a society's nervous system, rather than against its fielded forces, necessarily blurs the distinction between civilian and military objectives. The most important targets have a dual use. Television stations transmit military signals as well as information. Power stations run military computers as well as water pumping stations and hospitals. There is no guarantee that war directed at the nervous system of a society will be any less savage than war directed only at its troops.

Precision guidance was only the first element of the revolution in military affairs. The second was provided by computers. When linked up to surveillance satellites as well as spy planes, computers increase the information available to a commander and if – a big if – this information can be digested and compressed into timely knowledge of the enemy's dispositions, computers can improve a commander's capacity to react and anticipate in real time. Computers also improve coordination among military units and separate military services. In theory this ought to make it easier to mount joint operations from land, sea, air and space. If all the intelligence and command elements of the separate forces can be combined in a 'system of systems' the commander-in-chief could co-ordinate the actions of all his forces in near-perfect knowledge of the battle-space. Such at any rate is the theory.[12]

In practice, of course, technologies create possibilities, but whether they are exploited depends on the ability of essentially conservative institutions to embrace them. The revolution in military affairs has aroused intense resistance in the U.S. armed forces. The new technology seems to accuse generations' worth of procurement decisions. If you have Cruise missiles, why do you need all those airplanes? If you have precision guided weapons launched from submarines, why do you need all those aircraft carriers and destroyers? The new technology called into question the heavy industrial armies created to fight World War II. In effect, the RMA rang the curtain down on a century of total war – and on the military forces, which survived fifty years of peace by evoking its memory.

As the Cold War ended and the military irrelevance of World War II military forces became apparent, electorates began demanding a peace dividend. The new military technology seemed to offer politicians a way to cut back defense budgets without reducing military preparedness, by increasing the lethality of the military machine while sharply reducing its size and cost.[13] In the decade after 1989, the American armed services shed 36 percent of their personnel, and the percentage of gross domestic product devoted to defense fell from 6 to 3 percent.[14]

Faced with revolutionary change, military forces at first behaved according to the adage of the nineteenth-century Italian aristocracy, immortalized in Giuseppe Di Lampedusa's novel, *The Leopard*: 'If we want everything to remain as it is, it will be necessary for everything to change.' The military embraced the new technology, hoping thereby that the old World War II force structures could remain in place.

Each service wanted new technology provided it didn't have to sacrifice service traditions and jobs. The air force saw itself as an elite of pilots: plane-flying is the core of its mystique, and hence the force resisted unmanned aircraft and reconnaissance drones, even though these are substantially cheaper to fly and they save the lives of pilots. The navy held onto its carriers and destroyers and resisted the introduction of an arsenal ship, which is manned by a relatively small number of technicians who direct the firing of unmanned precision-guided munitions.[15]

The most entrenched resistance to the revolution in military affairs came from within the army. The navy could turn itself into a Cruise missile platform; the air force could turn itself into the high-altitude specialists of the age of precision weaponry. The U.S. Marines could re-equip themselves as the nation's emergency force: a sea-based expeditionary unit trained for embassy protection, relief assistance and seizing beachheads. But what would be the purpose of the army, of all those tanks, artillery pieces and that massive divisional structure inherited from World War II? The best thinkers in the army – and it is full of embattled intellectuals – realized that new technologies signaled the end of the divisional structure of the army, and the huge logistical support system it was forced to drag behind it. The new thinkers agreed that the army was a dinosaur, but they could not decide what new beast – light, lethal and mobile – was best equipped to take its place.

Strategic thinkers in the army also had to rebut the presumption that technology did away with the need for leadership and a warrior class.[16] For the central claim of the new technological gospel was that computers, battlefield sensors and spy satellites could dispel the 'fog' of war – the chaotic uncertainty in which battles unfold; and eliminate the 'friction' – adverse terrain, climate, equipment failure, troop morale and other incalculable factors – standing in the way of military victory. Generals like Norman Schwarzkopf were skeptical: they had bitter combat experience of both fog and friction in Vietnam.[17] They also knew that the 'systems analysts' of the Pentagon had promised then that new technologies married to new tactics – the Huey helicopter re-equipped as a gunship – would dispel the fog and grease the friction of warfare. And they hadn't.

Vietnam veterans like Schwarzkopf were also angered by the argument, made by some advocates of RMA, that putting troops on the ground was no longer necessary. Cruise missiles, these veterans maintained, could not hope to reverse invasions, like Saddam Hussein's occupation of Kuwait. Sooner or later, they argued, the army would need to put its soldiers on the ground to fight their way in and take and hold ground.

But even if this was true – and it most certainly was – the

problem was to identify the expeditionary force needed to fight the new enemies of the post-Cold War era. The Gulf War had vindicated the need to put combat troops on the ground but it was also clear that the Gulf War was a one-off. What other opponent was likely to allow America and its allies six un-opposed months to build up and deploy its forces? The Gulf War exposed the potential vulnerability of the American logistical back-up and the Army's elephantine slowness in deploying troops into combat. Future opponents would not give anyone this kind of time, or leave the logistical build-up unopposed.

In theory, RMA could solve all of these problems. Borrowing lessons learned from FedEx and UPS, the military could speed up the delivery of logistics, while improvements in precision weapons could reduce the amount of ammunition which expeditionary units would have to carry with them. In any event, the Army would no longer have to go in alone. The new era would mean an end to single-service deployments. All future expeditionary task forces would combine attack elements from the Navy, Air Force and Army. Improvements in computerization would make it possible to co-ordinate these elements into a genuinely combined force.

The new joint expeditionary force would have a flat command structure, allowing substantial initiative at the squad or platoon level. In the 1990s the US Marines developed the concept of the 'strategic corporal', a squad leader with sufficient operational autonomy and sufficient communications power at his fingertips to call in air strikes at a keystroke.[18] Improved command and control of forces in the field would also transform tactics.[19] The essential function of ground troops would no longer be to roll over the enemy in a traditional battle of attrition, but to maneuver, outflank and call in fire in order to overwhelm opposing forces. These sources of fire-power would no longer be on the battlefield, but at a distance: in submarines, helicopters, airplanes, long-range artillery, even satellites in space. With these assets on call, it would be possible to deploy soldiers without the array of battlefield artillery and tanks once required to protect them. Since this 'lightened up' the force, it would speed up their deployment. And speed is of the essence, to deter potential aggressors, and to gain the advantages of surprise and battlefield position.

The new tactics made possible by RMA were plain for all to see, but on the eve of the Kosovo war, however, the U.S. Army was still not ready to adopt them. It remained locked in an outdated divisional structure and force profile more adapted to D-Day than to the light expeditionary wars of the 1990s. It was still not able to put together a rapid reaction force capable of deploying to the borders of Kosovo quickly enough to dissuade Milosevic from attempting to expel the Albanian population and to repel him if he tried.

When recourse to force became inevitable, in January 1999, there was no longer time to deploy sufficient troops to deter. And even if the troops had been there, it is not clear that the Americans could have won an offensive ground war in mountainous conditions against the small decentralized units of the Serbian army and military police. Kosovo occurred, in other words, in mid-revolution. America dominates space; dominates the skies; but it does not dominate the ground. It has not yet re-organized its troops around the strategic doctrine which the revolution in military affairs makes possible: air-lifted maneuver-based warfare by lightly armed squads, working in and around enemy lines, to call in high precision fires from naval and space based assets.[20] One reason why ground forces were not committed in Kosovo was that the U.S. lacked the type of joint, mobile, rapidly deployable expeditionary force necessary for the task. And even if such a force had been available, in the new political climate in which Western nations go to war, the military cost of a ground operation would always have seemed prohibitively high. To some extent, America and its NATO allies fought a virtual war because they were neither ready nor willing to fight a real one.

3. *Virtual Consent*

While the American army's inability to fight mobile expeditionary wars forced the war into the skies, politics limited the kind of war that could be waged.

The power to give or withhold consent to war is an essential element of the freedom of citizens. War and defense remain the ultimate rationale of nation states. One of the dubious clichés of our time is that globalization is undermining this rationale.[21] A new interdependence might be emerging in the economic realm, but there is no discernible alternative to the nation state as the chief provider of foreign and domestic security for human populations. Commerce may be borderless, but human beings cannot be. They need secure territories to live in, and these can only be provided by states with monopolies over the legitimate use of force. It is difficult to imagine any global, regional or continental body replacing the state in these functions, because these bodies lack the democratic legitimacy required if citizens are to be sent to kill and to die.

Our constitutions provide that when our countries go to war, our leaders should make a declaration of war and seek approval for that declaration from our elected representatives in the Congress or Houses of Parliament. For the better part of fifty years – since the Korean War – these constitutional procedures have been bypassed. Western soldiers have been sent into armed conflict many times in the past decades – Panama, Haiti, Iraq, Somalia, Bosnia, and now Kosovo – and never once have their legislatures actually declared war. The War Powers Act of the United States remains a dead letter, as do the constitutional provisions for war-making in most nations.[22]

This bypassing of the constitution is assisted by linguistic subterfuge. Since constitutions state that war requires a declaration to be legitimate, the word 'war' never passes a leader's lips. As military expert Anthony Cordesman has wryly noted, 'one of the lessons of modern war is that war can no longer be called war.'[23] Instead in Kosovo, our leaders spoke of strikes and coercive diplomacy. In practice, of course, we were at war: our forces were taking and returning fire. In this fashion, linguistic subterfuge helped turn the real into the virtual.

In place of Congress and Parliament as the effective control on the war-making powers of our executives, we have polls and focus groups. Using these tools, a leader's political advisers craft an appeal for military action in words calculated to attract support. The word 'humanitarian' figures prominently. Leaders then address their electorates and afterwards pollsters consult samples of citizens to see just how far they support what the leader has in mind. The process has an element of circularity: citizens will endorse those military risks a leader is prepared to take, and a leader will propose only those risks which he believes his electorate will approve. In principle, citizens are usually more cautious than leaders, since they are the ones who have to do the fighting. When leaders call for more risk than an electorate will support, the polls pull them back into line.

Left to themselves most political leaders in the post-Cold War era would have avoided the political risks of military intervention if they could. They were driven to it by small yet vocal constituencies who succeeded in raising the political costs of standing by and doing nothing. In the Balkan wars of the 1990s, the American President was under constant pressure from a determined and influential band of opinion-formers – writers, editors, reporters, Balkans experts, members of the Washington bureaucracy, Congressmen and Senators – who articulated both moral and strategic reasons for military intervention. What a British Foreign Secretary dismissed as the 'something must be done brigade' ended up having a decisive impact in forcing the NATO political and military elites into action. This call for intervention was bipartisan: it mobilized conservatives and liberals, Republicans and Democrats in a politics of outrage. They played, above all, on a widely shared sense of disquiet, within the Administration, at its failure to stop the shelling of Sarajevo, to curb the Serb-led attempt to destroy the internationally recognized state of Bosnia-Hercegovina and to halt the ethnic cleansing of Bosnia which resulted in the death of 200,000 people and the deportation of several million inhabitants.[24] This was shame, it should be said, not guilt; embarrassment at the palpable failure of leadership rather than any sense of culpability for the lives destroyed through presidential inaction. Bosnia made it perfectly plain that there were substantial costs to a presidential reputation if a commander-in-chief stood by while massacre occurred. But again, if shame had a political cost, it did so because it found articulation by a vocal minority of influential activists – with access to the media.

This minority was vocal but its support was shallow. Isolationist exceptionalism – the sense of the United States being a city on a hill, safe from the fratricide of Europe – runs deep in the American electorate.[25] The shame of Bosnia – like that of Kosovo – was not widely or deeply felt in domestic opinion. From the beginning, the political dynamics in favor of intervention were much weaker than the op-ed columns and discussions on television shows implied. A risk-averse President, consummate in his ability to follow rather than lead, was reluctant to go as far as the interventionist constituency wanted him to.

Of course, intervention posed huge risks. Any political leader worth his salt knows that military operations rarely turn out as predicted, and citizens – who often have military experience of their own – know that wars are a fearful lottery. Both sides – leader and led – must take a gamble. The electorate's trust is conditional and liable to rupture if the military action runs into those unintended consequences – death, disaster and failure – which both leaders and led know are possible. The uncertainty inherent in all decisions about going to war drives both leaders and citizens to err on the side of caution. So, in the case of Kosovo the American President ruled out ground troops, committing America to intervention only if impunity could be guaranteed.

But if war in the future is sold to voters with the promise of impunity they may be tempted to throw caution to the winds. If military action is cost-free, what democratic restraints will remain on the resort to force? New weaponry may force us to re-assess an essential assumption about democracies: that they go to war less frequently than authoritarian regimes, and that they rarely, if ever, go to war against fellow democracies. Democracies may well remain peace loving only so long as the risks of war remain real to their citizens. If war becomes virtual

– and without risk – democratic electorates may be more willing to fight especially if the cause is justified in the language of human rights and even democracy itself.

In this emerging regime of virtual consent, the public is consulted but the formal institutions of democracy are by-passed. These new human rights wars are occurring just when the influence of representative institutions on the conduct of war and peace is declining. These institutions survive, but they are increasingly perfunctory. Our representatives debate in empty chambers, and in the supposedly ultimate questions of war and peace, leaders go over the heads of representatives to mold and manipulate public opinion directly. As a result, the checks and balances of constitutional government – one of whose central purposes is to restrain an intemperate or ill-considered use of military force by the executive power – fall into abeyance. Those who favor military intervention are apt to dismiss this problem, indeed to praise prime ministers and presidents for mobilizing popular support for military action over the heads of habitually isolationist or doubting legislatures. But interventions which do not obtain the consent of legislatures are apt to lose sustaining political support at the first sign of military trouble.

Moreover, formal debates in representative bodies subject military aims to the kind of detailed scrutiny they cannot expect to receive through opinion polling. The institutional checks and balances of a democratic system help, in other words, to clarify the goals and purposes of war. When military operations are unsanctioned and undeclared, as they were in Kosovo, their objectives changed from week to week, depending on what our leaders decided they should be. At first, citizens were asked only to support a limited air campaign designed to force a recalcitrant regime back to the negotiating table. Within days, the military objective had expanded into an all-out crusade to stop and reverse ethnic cleansing. Even when the ambit of operations widened out, the public was never told what kind of result was being sought. If war aims had been subject to formal debate in the legislatures of the NATO countries, it is possible, for example, that a more rigorous attempt to protect the Serbian and Roma minorities would have been made once entry to Kosovo had been achieved.

The decay of institutional checks and balances on the war-making power of the executive has received almost no attention in the debate over the Kosovo conflict. This suggests that citizens no longer even care whether their elected politicians exercise their constitutional responsibilities. Populist cynicism toward the political process has gone so far that we no longer even notice that the institutions which exist to protect our liberties are not doing their job. We have allowed ourselves to accept virtual consent in the most important political matter of all: war and peace.

The only issue of political legitimacy to arouse discussion has been the failure of the NATO allies to seek Security Council approval for the use of military force under Chapter VII of the UN Charter. It is a further sign of the weakness of our democracy that the one question we should ask of the legality of war is why it did not receive approval from an international institution which, important as it is, does not actually commit the troops which fight the battles.

Intervention in Kosovo was justified at the UN on the grounds that urgent necessity over-rode the requirement of formal consent, which in any case could not have been achieved in the face of the Chinese and Soviet veto. When a house is on fire, you do not seek a search warrant before entering to put out the blaze. This argument drew on the UN's experience in Rwanda, where impasse and inaction in the Security Council led to the needless deaths of a million people.[26] This argument from necessity has merit, but there is no doubt that failure to secure formal approval further undermined the legitimacy of the military operation. All of the opposition to the war throughout the world focused on NATO's failure to abide by the letter of the Charter. The claim that its spirit was being respected was convincing to those who made it, but sounded like an argument from *force majeure* to everyone else.

One lesson of the conflict is that there needs to be a renewal of both national and international institutions with the power to ratify the decision to go to war. In the case of national parliaments, committee powers of review must be strengthened and legislatures must insist that military operations receive their formal approval. In the case of the UN, the Security Council must be reformed; enlarged so that it can become more representative of the world's populations and restructured so as to replace the veto system of the Permanent Five with majority voting. Such reform is exceedingly unattractive to the great powers and hence unlikely to happen, but whether or not it is a realistic proposition, the arguments in principle for it – and even the advantages of it to the Permanent Five – should be made clear. All modern military operations need international legitimacy if they are going to succeed. Consequently, the great powers, especially America, face a difficult choice: they can either maintain their veto, and embark on unsanctioned military adventures with their partners only to see these fail because they lack international approval; or they can surrender veto power in return for the increased likelihood of securing majority approval for the use of military power.

Institutional reform is necessary at both the domestic and international level, yet no set of institutional safeguards can ever protect democracies from unwise military adventure. Since war is, by definition, an uncertain gamble, no leader, however responsible, can fully advise his citizens of its dangers. In the Kosovo case, the public did not sign up to 78 days' worth of bombing, and had they been asked, most would have said No, as we can judge from the steady decline in public support for bombing as it proceeded. What the public signed up for – to the degree that they were asked at all – was a military operation to save the Kosovar Albanians from ethnic cleansing. But the President secured the public's consent by withholding the indubitable fact, attested by his military commanders, that ethnic cleansing could only be deterred or stopped by ground troops. As a consequence, the intervention provided Serbia with the opportunity to perpetrate the worst act of ethnic cleansing in Europe this decade.

There is no knowing, of course, whether this debacle could have been avoided if democracy had worked, if Congress or Parliament had subjected the executive's war-making plans to the kind of scrutiny which would have exposed this gap between means and ends. It is even possible that legislatures might have refused to endorse any intervention at all. Fearing that legislatures would never support them anyway, the constituency in favour of intervention is uninterested in the decay of legislative scrutiny of war and peace. A strong and unencumbered executive seems to work in favor of their interests. Yet those in favor of intervention should be concerned that they depend for action on an executive which manipulates the consent of the governed, instead of seeking genuine democratic approval. The same executive power which authorized a Kosovo intervention today also authorized Vietnam and El Salvador yesterday. The day will surely come when the executive will seek to intervene somewhere in the name of human rights and do so in a fashion which violates or traduces the principles it purports to defend. Then, our democracies may be too weak to save themselves from disgrace.

4. Virtual Mobilization

In virtual war, citizens are not only divested of their power to give consent. They are also demobilized. We now wage wars and few notice or care. War no longer demands the type of physical involvement or moral attention it required over the past two centuries.

War has been associated with mass mobilization since the first French Revolutionary army of the 1790s. Until then command of troops had been an aristocratic pastime and soldiering had been a mercenary occupation. The French revolutionary armies transformed war from a battle between dynasties into a confrontation between peoples, requiring the mobilization of a nation's entire population.[27] France's soldiers were defending something new – *La France*, a nation of citizens. They went to war to carry the values of that nation – liberty equality and fraternity to captive peoples across Europe. The citizen became a soldier, and military sacrifice became the highest form of civic virtue.

Where France led, the rest of Europe followed. But it was only in the twentieth century that the relation between democratic citizenship, mass mobilization and total war was taken to its extreme conclusion. World War I was a fight to the death between populations. Total mobilization proved to be a malign consequence of the marriage between democracy and nationalism: if all are citizens, all must serve; if a nation is attacked, all her sons must defend her; if asked, all must sacrifice themselves.

In the total wars of the twentieth century, mobilization of the population sank deep roots in the psyche, helping to define the ideals of masculine and feminine identity and connecting masculinity with the idea of the upright carriage of the drill-yard, the coarse jocularity of the barracks and strict self-control in the face of danger and death. Military ideals of discipline – vertical, hierarchical, unquestioning – exerted an influence well beyond military life – in school, prison and factory.[28]

War also dominated the economies of the West: demand for armaments helped create the mass production factory. In turn, the state's management of the economy in wartime created the precedent – a false one, as it turned out – for attempts to run the economy in the same way in peacetime. Socialism as an ideal appealed strongly to sentimentalized memories of collective effort in wartime. If we could work together to beat the enemy, so the reasoning went, why couldn't we pull together in peacetime? War mobilization created the model for Lenin's War Communism in Russia and for more democratic variants of the command economy in Western Europe. It is no accident that the high-water marks of European socialism occurred immediately after the First and Second World Wars.[29]

Wartime mobilization also defined the national identity of the European nations. War – the heroic resistance of a whole nation – became the central myths of at least two of the Western peoples: Russia and Great Britain; and military defeat became the great enduring shame of two others: France and Germany. Either way, war penetrated the identity of the

185

citizen, just as it defined the ultimate purpose of the state.

We cannot understand the deliriously happy crowds who greeted the onset of war in 1914 unless we appreciate that the general mobilization offered them a moment of ecstatic moral communion with fellow citizens. Moreover, to the degree that these crowds could anticipate the bloodshed that lay ahead, they did so within a framework of assumptions radically different from our own. The bloody sacrifices of war were somewhat easier to accept in societies used to high infant mortality and the unchecked scourges of illness and disease. Death on the battlefield was less of a scandal to societies in which death was a daily fact of life. In cultures that still soldered the identity of the individual and the identity of the nation together in the idea of the 'ultimate sacrifice' death in battle retained its glory. All of this is now far distant. At the Marine's Iwo Jima Memorial, Charles Jagger's brooding tribute to the Royal Artillery at Hyde Park Corner in London or in the Canadian memorial at Vimy Ridge, we see an affirmation of sacrifice which seems both utterly without irony and utterly remote.[30]

Sacrifice in battle has become implausible or ironic in the course of the twentieth century as the gulf between military and civilian values has grown. To some extent, this reflects the gradual banishment of death as the over-riding pre-occupation of civilian society. As infant mortality has declined, as life expectancy has increased, as peace has become a settled expectation of civilian populations, the idea of martial sacrifice and the nobility of death in combat have become ever more extreme destinies, now seen as increasingly implausible to cultures raised to count on a full adult life. The warrior has become an anomalous figure in what Edward Luttwak has called a post-heroic culture.[31]

The arrival of the nuclear era further weakened the martial ideal. By guaranteeing fifty years – and beyond – of uncertain yet durable peace, nuclear weapons slowly eroded the logic of mobilization for national defense. In the process, Europe and the United States began dismantling their conscript armies. Britain got rid of national service in the late 1950s; America abolished the draft in the 1970s. One month after victory in the Kosovo war Congress did away with the funding for maintaining a draft lottery in peacetime. France, which had begun the era of mass conscription with the *levée en masse* in the 1790s, announced that it would end conscription just before the Kosovo war.[32] The conflict occurred just as a very large parenthesis in the history of warfare was closing – the end of the two-hundred-year history of conscription, the mass mobilization of society which went with it and the idea of war as a trial of national survival.

When war ceases to be connected to national survival, it loses its reservoir of support among citizens. The fissure between war and vital national interest first became apparent in Vietnam.[33] The longer the war went on – in the name of values, it should be remembered, defending a small 'democratic' country against invasion from the communist north – the less defensible it seemed to the American public. It is often said that the public's disaffection was the work of television news.[34] Wars whose consequences are visible are unsustainable in the long term. Once citizens know what war looks like, once they see the black body-bags lined up on the helicopter landing pads, their taste for foreign military adventure is bound to evaporate. Yet war does not become illegitimate simply because citizens see carnage on their screens. It becomes illegitimate when the political reasons for it no longer convince. The Vietnam war was made unsustainable by the doubt that the Anti-War campaign lodged in the minds of the political elite, a doubt reinforced by the tenacity of the North Vietnamese.

The American public and its military came away from Vietnam unwilling to shed blood in wars unconnected with essential national interests. The debacle in Vietnam also brought the draft to an end, and the result has widened the gulf between civilian and military culture. When citizens cease to train as warriors, they no longer share a common memory of basic training, boot camp, maneuvers and war. Masculinity has slowly emancipated itself from the warrior ideal. The warrior has become a full-time professional and the values which the military seek to inculcate – honor, courage, sacrifice, love of country – here diverged from the values rewarded in the civilian economy. Over time, military values command less automatic assent in society, with the result that they have become increasingly politicized. Sensing their alienation from the American mainstream in the 1980s, the officer class has entered the political struggle to re-orient the country back to fundamentals.[35] Post Vietnam America has been a battle-ground between religious and secular, liberal and conservative value systems, and in this battle, most of the officer elite has aligned with conservative, Republican and religious interests. Many career soldiers both fear and regret the politicization of the officer corps, but the trend is clear.[36] In America, the dominant ethos of the military elite has become ever more Christian, conservative, Republican in politics, and southern and mid-western in origin.[37] There is little communion between them and the largely liberal and secular circles who sustain most demands for humanitarian and human rights interventions.

The Nineties has seen the retirement of political leaders with direct experience of World War II or Vietnam and the emergence of a political elite that no longer has personal experience of the warrior's trade. The military consequently suspects their political superiors; and politicians do not feel comfortable with their military. In a society increasingly distant from the culture of war, the rhetoric politicians use to mobilize their populations in support of military operations becomes unreal and insincere. As commanders-in-chief of their armed forces, Presidents and Prime Ministers are required to use a language saturated with military values: sacrifice, honor, courage. But to leaders and voters who have never gone to war, these phrases have a nostalgic, inauthentic feel and the consensus that the rhetoric creates is bound to be skin-deep – vulnerable to military adversity or bad luck.

As war loses its hold over national identity and the language of patriotism, it is also losing its role in the economy of advanced states. In times past, wars could bankrupt societies, and economic constraints were a fundamental limit on the length and ferocity of conflict. These economic limits are in the process of disappearing for an advanced society like America. The US may spend $230 billion a year on its defense, an enormous figure by the standards of any other nation, but only 3 percent of its gross domestic product.[38] The military industrial complex may have bulked large in the economy at the end of World War II, and even throughout the 1960s. But in the new post-industrial, computer-based economy of the 1980s and 90s, the military mobilizes far fewer resources than before.

Moreover, the terms of trade between the military and civilian spheres have been reversed. In the industrial era, war was a major engine of technical innovation, and defense expenditure drove the economy. Many of the innovations which made possible the computer revolution – the Internet and encryption, to take but two examples – originated in the military-industrial complex and were passed onto the domestic sector. In the post-industrial era, the private economy leads and the military follows – buying off-the-shelf computer hardware and software or adapting the computerized tracking systems used by commercial delivery companies to streamline cumbersome military logistics. The once-powerful American intelligence community is now unable to compete with private companies in the development of new encryption software; nor can it recruit the most talented programmers into military service.[39] When the Marines go to Wall Street to learn about decision-making under stress, and when the military turns to Wal-Mart to learn about logistics – the era of military mobilization of the civilian economy is well and truly over.[40]

Post-industrial warfare does not require the conversion of enterprises from private to public management or the creation of vast defense industries. Even as large an operation as Desert Storm exerted only a moderate impact upon the private economy or the public budget. American society takes this kind of military operation in its stride. No trade-off between guns and butter has to be made. War no longer faces society with painful choices. It ceases to be associated with the idea of economic sacrifice.

Since war no longer reaches into the civilian economy and mobilizes everything in its path, the conflicts of the future may take place without anyone even realizing they are occurring. Indeed, since 1998, US and British air forces have been flying punitive bombing missions over Iraq, directed at maintaining a no-fly zone over Iraqi Kurdistan, disabling Iraq's air-defense system and preventing the Iraqi regime from restoring its military capability. The tonnage of explosive unleashed upon Iraq approaches the tonnage unleashed on Kosovo but since our pilots are not at substantial risk, and the action seems more of a holding operation than anything else, the media scarcely bothers to report what is in fact a real conflict. Its unreality even seeps into the pilots' consciousness. As one of them told a journalist, 'Having somebody shoot at me . . . makes me feel like I'm at war.'[41] Wars that do not mobilize societies do not seem quite real even to those who fight them.

War thus becomes virtual, not simply because it appears to take place on a screen but because it enlists societies only in virtual ways. Due to nuclear weapons, it is no longer a struggle for national survival; with the end of conscription, it no longer requires the actual participation of citizens; because of the bypassing of representative institutions, it no longer requires democratic consent; and as a result of the exponential growth of the modern economy, it no longer draws on the entire economic system. These conditions transform war into something like a spectator sport. As with sports, nothing ultimate is at stake: neither national survival, nor the fate of the economy. War affords the pleasures of a spectacle, with the added thrill that it is real for someone, but not, happily, for the spectator.

6. Media War

When war becomes a spectator sport, the media becomes the decisive theater of operations. If the consensus in favor of humanitarian intervention can be shaken – as it was in Somalia – by the sight of a single American serviceman's body being dragged through the streets of Mogadishu, then keeping those images off the screen becomes a central objective of the military art.[42]

The presence of cameras in the field of operations does more than exert a constraint on military actions. It changes the focus of hostilities from the enemy's fielded forces to the civilian opinion at home which sustains the will to fight. Here America revealed its vulnerability. Since the end of the Cold War no opponent of the United States has had the means to resist its power. The only viable responses have been asymmetrical, aimed not at military objectives per se, but at American public opinion: terrorism against civilian targets or American installations abroad, cyberwar against U.S. computer systems; and most important of all, media war.[43] After the first night of Desert Storm, Saddam Hussein lost his air-defense against allied aviation over Baghdad, but he did have an exceedingly powerful weapon in his arsenal – the media – and he did not have to wait long to use it. As soon as the Amiriyeh Bunker was hit by US Stealth bombers on February 13, 1991, he invited Western TV crews to film the carnage. The American claim that it had been a legitimate military target – a command and control bunker – became irrelevant once it was revealed that three hundred women and children from families of the military elite had sheltered there and had been incinerated.[44] The Iraqi regime is not notably concerned for the lives of women and children – witness its chlorine gas attack on the Kurdish city of Halabja in 1988 – but it understood immediately that its best chance of stopping the air bombardment of Baghdad lay in getting the cameras in.[45] And so it proved. The pictures of the carnage had the desired effect. Western opinion reacted against the bombing, and it was immediately curtailed.

In the Kosovo war, likewise, the Milosevic regime knew that

its outdated air-defense system at best could force NATO to fly above 15,000 feet. It stood little chance of actually shooting down NATO bombers and cruise missiles. The regime seized instead on the only available asymmetrical response: to use Western media to exploit grisly incidents and undermine popular support for the war at home. Western television crews duly reported the bombing of the Serbian television station, the Serbian socialist party headquarters, the train on the bridge, the refugee convoys in Kosovo. More than any other factor, this reportage sowed doubt in the minds of a Western electorate that had been in favor of military action when the bombing began. By the end of the operation, poll support for further bombing slipped below 50 percent for the first time, and it is doubtful that military action could have been continued much longer than it was.

This aspect of war is historically new: there were no Allied reporters in Berlin, Hamburg or Dresden when they were bombed; there were no German journalists covering the Allied side of the trenches in World War I. The conduct of war has become more transparent in the past 75 years, and the distance between home and the battlefield has diminished, like all the distances in our world. But this does not merely mean that we see war in a new way; it also transforms journalists from observers into protagonists, and makes the media much more than mediators. In virtual war, journalists are turned, willingly or otherwise, into combatants. Western journalists in Belgrade were faced with difficult choices: if they went on Serb-organized tours of NATO attack sites and reported what was presented to them as true, they risked being seen as dupes of the Serbian regime; if they refused, they risked deportation, or what was worse, losing the pictures to their competitors. In the circumstances, journalists found themselves exploited by both sides in the conflict. NATO attempted to manipulate the press into believing that alliance cohesion was being maintained and that the bombing was working. The Serbian regime attempted to use the Western media to erode domestic political support. The public at home did its best to decode the messages they were receiving and to winnow out the small grain of truth from the chaff of disinformation on both sides.

The attack on the Serbian television station illustrates just how complex and dark the truth could be. In peacetime, disgruntled citizens of Serbia did discount much of Serbian television output as propaganda on behalf of an unpopular regime. In wartime conditions of censorship and alarm, they rallied to its message. The NATO command sought to strike the television system in order to weaken Milosevic's capacity to communicate with his domestic support, and secondarily to put the transmitters out of action as military relays.

The strike raised difficult issues, because it seemed to be an attack on the media itself – on freedom of speech – and therefore would be unpopular with the Western media. Within the NATO command, allies were at loggerheads, with British lawyers arguing that the Geneva Conventions prohibit the targeting of journalists and television stations, and the American side maintaining that the supposed 'hate speech' broadcast by the station foreclosed its legal immunity under the conventions. This made the curious argument that the inviolability of journalists is conditional on the content of what they broadcast.

While these disputes were proceeding, the Western public was prepared for the strikes by daily NATO briefings which characterized the TV station as a dual use target, transmitting both hate speech and military signals. By the time the target was struck, public opinion had been extensively prepared by Western background briefers.[46] This too is a new development. In real wars of the past, belligerents concealed their intentions. In virtual war, on the contrary, both sides broadcast them. In real war, belligerents seek to inflict real damage; in virtual war, both sides seek to inflict perceptual damage in order to undermine civilian morale.

The Serbs had only to look at the broadcast of the daily NATO briefings to Western journalists to realise that the television station was a likely target. And when Western news crews, who made use of the building for editing and trans- mission of footage, were warned to keep clear of the building on the day of the proposed attack, Serb officials deduced that an attack was imminent. Why then were 15 people – including non-essential personnel like a young female make-up artist on duty when the Stealth bomber struck? In the case of the Ministry of Defense and the Military Police Headquarters in Belgrade, the NATO briefings had indicated that these were targets and they were cleared of personnel days before the attack. Many media workers in Belgrade suspect that the television authorities ordered their staff to remain in the building, knowing full well that it was about to be attacked. Why? In order to create an incident which could be used to sway Western opinion against the bombing. And why the TV station? Because of all targets, it was the one which, if hit, would create most adverse reaction among the Western media.[47] And so it proved. Indeed the only way to explain why the station was struck and the risks were run is that Western commanders wanted to prove that they would not be deterred by such criticism. The bombing was a demonstration of ruthlessness in a war that had given Serbia more than a few occasions to doubt NATO's resolve.

The omnipresence and power of the media encourage the belief that the truth in these matters will eventually come out. In the Kosovo campaign, NATO never enjoyed total control of the press because to do so, it would have had to ban journalist travel to Serbia and this would have fallen foul of the free speech traditions of Western society. In the Gulf War and the Falklands campaigns, on the other hand, where access to the battlefield depended entirely on the military, movement of journalists was used successfully to control their reporting. In their war of reconquest in Chechnya, the Russians have shown themselves adept at banning or restricting access to the battle-field to both journalists and aid workers. Closing off the battlefield gives commanders the leeway to bombard civilians as they please. The supposed transparency of modern wars is a fiction. Wars fought on and for television – virtual wars – will not be less violent and destructive than those fought before the age of the television camera.

Future wars may even escape the scrutiny of journalists and observers altogether. If the target is the enemy's computer or banking infrastructure and the only weapons are computer viruses, no one will know the war is being fought until it is over. This kind of war will present a real challenge to the vigilance and persistence of the media and citizens as well.

Truth is always a casualty in war, but in virtual war, the media creates the illusion that what we are seeing is true. In reality, nothing is what it seems. Atrocities are not necessarily atrocities. Victories are not necessarily victories. Damage is not necessarily 'collateral'. But these deceptions have become intrinsic to the art of war. Virtual war is won by being spun. In these circumstances, a good citizen is a highly suspicious one.

7. The Legal War

Because virtual wars are fought on camera and are directed primarily at the opponent's will to fight, Western military commanders know that success is now contingent on public acceptance. In fact, there is no such thing as purely military success: a strike which takes out a target but leaves behind moral or political debris is a strike which has failed. The Western military's response to sharpened moral and political exposure has been to call in the lawyers. Commanders have concluded that they must have their targets vetted for moral and legal suitability before they launch their air-crews. The consequence has been an extraordinary growth in the power and influence of military lawyers at every level of the targeting and deployment process. A recent history of the Judge Advocate General's department – the American military lawyers charged with bringing prosecutions for violations of the US uniform military code of justice and the Geneva Conventions – shows that military lawyers had no place whatever in the targeting decisions in the air war over Vietnam in the 1960s. By 1989, when the United States invaded Panama, military lawyers were offering legal advice on a variety of issues from avoiding intrusions into Cuban airspace to restitution of seized civilian property. By 1991 concerns about maintaining the legitimacy of coalition warfare in the Gulf brought military lawyers into the planning of the air and ground wars.[48] By 1999, military lawyers had been integrated into every phase of the air campaign, including the finalization of the air-tasking orders which assigned pilots to specific targets and missions. Military lawyers, attached to United States European Command, sat at computer terminals and contributed assessments of the standard Geneva Convention questions for each target: was the objective military; were the means selected proportional to the objective; and what were the risks of damage to civilians. The texts of the Geneva Conventions themselves were available on screen.[49]

Such legal input has led to a veritable casuistry of war thanks to new technology. Precision reconnaissance photography – from satellites, unarmed drones and manned aircraft – linked to global positioning satellites have made it possible for lawyers and targeting specialists to distinguish individual parts of buildings from others. So that in the case of the Serbian TV strike, two blocks of the complex which housed secretarial or administrative staff were excluded from the strike. The studio block alone was hit – in the belief that this would take the station off the air. Improvements in the science of ballistics, and in modeling of explosive impacts, enabled weaponeers to predict, with unprecedented accuracy, what spray of damage a particular weapon was likely to cause. Every single one of the more than 500 targets in Kosovo was subjected to this type of review.

This process was not foolproof, but what is significant is that the mistakes – the bombing of refugee convoys, the targeting of the civilian train, the Chinese embassy – were *seen* as mistakes.[50] Legal war, when linked to precision weaponry and targeting, creates an expectation, which military, public and politicians alike come to share, that war can be clean and mistake free. This utopian expectation is fuelled by the marriage of legal analysis to precision guided weapons. Their use is increasing with every new conflict. In 1991, at the time of the Gulf War, precision guided munitions amounted to no more than 8 percent of the ordnance dropped on Iraq. In 1999, precision ordnance had risen to 35 percent.[51] But legal imperatives combined with public expectation are driving warfare towards 100 percent precision weapon use. And in the near future, precision-guidance technologies will be applied to small arms as well as large missiles and bombs.[52] If you have the capacity to discriminate, so the argument runs, you incur the moral obligation to do so. In future, it is easy to envisage that the Geneva Conventions will be re-written in order to permit the sanction of states who have precision weapons, or even non-lethal ones, and fail to use them.[53]

Given that lawyers have infiltrated every decision-making arena in modern society, from hospitals to the Oval Office, it is inevitable that they should have infiltrated the military. They provide harried decision-makers with a critical guarantee of legal coverage, turning complex issues of morality into technical issues of legality, so that whatever moral or operational doubts a commander may have, he can at least be sure that he will not face legal consequences. The Geneva Conventions have become a casuist's bible, and close readings of their fine print are supposed to eliminate the moral and political risks associated with military violence. Yet moral questions stubbornly resist being reduced to legal ones, and moral exposure is not eliminated when legal exposure is. No matter what the Geneva Conventions say, the targeting of a television or power station is bound to remain sensitive, and subtle legal defenses will not make it less so. Moreover, law does not necessarily create the grounds for consensus among allies. The French, British and Americans each took a different view of their potential exposure under the Geneva Conventions, and each instructed their air-crews to stay on the ground when missions they considered legally dubious were taking place.

This was not the only ambiguity in NATO's legal position. While conceding the principle of universal jurisdiction for crimes of war – indeed insisting that Serbia accept the jurisdiction of the International Criminal Tribunal in the Hague – the NATO military command was reluctant to accept that universal jurisdiction might apply to them, i.e. that their pilots too might come within the reach of the Tribunal for breaches of the laws of war. The Tribunal's right to try these pilots is clear enough, since the Security Council resolution establishing the Tribunal gives it jurisdiction over all combatants in the territory of the former Yugoslavia, regardless of nationality. NATO's military lawyers conceded this jurisdiction in theory, but denied it in practice, maintaining that their pilots would face justice at home, before national military tribunals and national military law. The question remains moot, of course, since no one on the NATO side has been indicted for violations of the laws of war but the contradictions in the NATO position are inescapable.[54]

Legal constraints are necessary if wars are to preserve public support. The real problem with the entry of lawyers into the prosecution of warfare is that it encourages the illusion that war is clean if the lawyers say so. A further illusion is that if we play by the rules, the enemy will too. Thus, Serbian forces deliberately dispersed command posts among concentrations of refugees in order to deter strikes from the air. Unable to counter American air power, Serbian forces waged war on the civilian population of Kosovo on the ground, correctly judging that American forces would not be deployed to stop them. The air campaign did not cause the ethnic cleansing, but there seems little doubt that Milosevic anticipated an air campaign and gambled that he could use it as a cover – and as a justification – for an attack on unprotected civilians. The lesson is clear: it is a form of hubris to suppose that the way we choose to wage war will determine how the other side fights. Our choice to wage 'clean' war may result in wars of exceptional dirtiness.

8. *Virtual Values*

Values are real to the degree that we are prepared to risk something in order to make them prevail. Values are virtual when they remain rhetorical, when the commitments we express are not followed with action. The language used to mobilize citizens to go to war – sacrifice, honor and country – is a virtual rhetoric, increasingly unreal to the citizenry on behalf of whom the military are sent. The same can be said of the language of values – human rights above all – used to justify military intervention in the first place.

It is often said by cynics that these values have never had anything but a rhetorical existence. But this is no longer so. These values – human rights especially – *have* acquired powerful institutional constituencies behind them. They have been imbedded in an interlocking structure of international treaties since 1945 and there is little doubt that they significantly abridge the freedom of states to abuse their own citizens at will. International conventions, ratified by most UN member states, are now enforced by a multitude of non-governmental organizations – from Amnesty International to Human Rights Watch – and by literally thousands of indigenous, local groups. Taken together, these changes amount to a revolution: they enfranchise the individual against the state for the first time in international law. What is generally conceded now – as it was not in the 1930s – is that states must abide by international human rights standards and the failure to do so can result in sanctions, 'naming and shaming' by international rights groups, and international isolation.[55]

The question is whether this revolution has established a *de facto* right of humanitarian intervention. Non-Western nations, especially Russia and China, insist that the UN Charter's presumption in favor of national sovereignty has not and should not be changed. But Western nations – especially NATO countries – have maintained, at least since the end of the Cold War, that they do have a warrant to intervene where breaches of human rights are flagrant and persistent, and where they constitute a threat to international peace and security. The Chinese and the Russians can withhold United Nations approval for military intervention, but short of threatening nuclear war, they cannot stop them, and in the nature of things, such interventions do not endanger their interests sufficiently to warrant the use of the nuclear threat.

So the limits on the West's use of military power for humanitarian missions are largely self-imposed. Although critics of American imperialism would deny it, these self-imposed limitations are substantial.[56] The most important of these is that democracies committed to self-determination cannot consistently deny self-determination to others. In practice, Western countries do not always live up to this injunction: Chilean self-determination under Allende was comprehensively subverted by American covert assistance to the Chilean military. But our own confessed requirement to live up to democratic principles renders such interventions the exception rather than the rule. The same commitment to self-determination rules out the use of force for conquest. We can drive oppressors out; but we are not entitled to use military force to acquire an empire or new pieces of territory. Nor do we believe ourselves to be entitled to use military power to change a regime by force. So our tanks did not go to Baghdad and our forces did not enter Belgrade.

Nothing so vividly reflects the extent to which modern

democracies defer to the ideal of self-determination as the notion that every intervention must have an 'exit strategy' – a plan to wrap up the engagement, withdraw with minimal loss and ensure continuity of military gains without committing troops of occupation. 'Exit strategies' would not have occurred to the Roman or the British Empires. Not so today. Western nations may still want to control and influence; but they no longer believe they have the right to rule. This self-limitation has both admirable and negative consequences. What is admirable is the determination to leave behind an imperial past. What is negative is that Western interventions do not last long enough to make a difference. Leaving aside the endemic inefficiency and even corruption of the UN and European organizations who have administered the short-lived protectorates of the post Cold War era – from Cambodia to Angola, from Bosnia to Kosovo – rebuilding these societies takes time, and it is time that Western states do not have. More than failure of will, these half-hearted protectorates reflect a conflict within our own principles: between commitments to human rights and to self-determination. Western states believe in defending human rights, but not at the price of taking territory to make these values prevail. This helps to explain the gap between the absolute character of the commitments made to justify military operations and the conditional means employed to back them up. In this gap between commitment and action lurks the problem of bad faith. Military force is credible only to the extent that the will that uses it is credible. Since self-doubt is always obvious to an enemy, it can negate the effect of superiority. If an opponent doubts our commitment to use force, we are then forced to use force, not in service of a strategic objective of our own choosing, but because our bluff has been called. Such was the case in Kosovo. Serbia gambled on our reticence, especially our unwillingness to risk casualties. Milosevic reasoned that, at worst, he would have to endure a relatively brief set of air strikes directed at his air defenses – on the model of the Balkan air operation in late August–early September 1995 which paved the way for the Dayton agreement.[57] If he could survive this, Milosevic reasoned, then he might be home free. The alliance would not have the stomach for ground operations, and if he were daring enough, he might even be able to drive the Kosovar Albanians from their homeland and end up, after several weeks, with NATO divided and humiliated and Serbia in possession of an ethnically cleansed Kosovo.

He made the wrong gamble – but the very fact that he considered gambling against overwhelming military force indicates the weakness of liberal democratic states when faced with determined opponents. They reason that the West's commitment to human rights is canceled out by its unwillingness to take casualties, and its commitment to help the vulnerable is canceled out by its unwillingness to take and hold territory.

But the Allied use of force – in such coerced circumstances – does not vindicate our credibility. It only makes our reluctance palpable. Thus, at the end of the Kosovo operation, the American Secretary of Defense had to re-state, yet again, that the fact that Americans took no casualties was not a sign that it was not prepared to take casualties in the future. William Cohen told the Senate Armed Services committee, 'There's a misapprehension that this is the goal of the United States, that this is a standard that has been set by the Pentagon, there can be no casualties incurred. I want to make sure that everybody understands, we are not setting a standard, did not set one here, that there should be no combat fatalities.'[58] These words are not exactly convincing. In real wars, victory ends arguments about credibility; in virtual wars, victory ends with credibility still in question. For these reasons, moral reticence in relation to the use of force may increase the propensity to use force. We keep waging war, not because we want to, but because we have seeded a doubt about our seriousness which only a concerted display of violence – which we wished to avoid – can eradicate.

9. Virtual Alliances

Another substantial constraint on the use of military power is the requirement of alliance support. Since Vietnam, the American elite has been aware of the dangers of going it alone in military affairs. The legitimacy of its military operations overseas depends on persuading other states to join as coalition partners. Indeed, coalition warfare is increasingly seen as the future of war. It is a sign of how much the political culture of international relations has changed in the era of the UN Charter that violence vested solely with the national interest of a single country is less likely to command the assent of the world than violence vested in a coalition of the willing.

In the Gulf War, military success depended on assembling a coalition which included Arab states. Without their participation, the operation would have been seen as an exercise in Western coercion. With Arab participation, its ostensible purpose – the eviction of an invader who had violated the sovereignty of a member state of the UN – became believable. Because it was believable, the Russians and other potential allies of the Iraqis saw no opportunity to support Saddam Hussein and win international kudos and influence by doing so. In this instance securing coalition legitimacy for military operations was a critical factor in their eventual success.

In Kosovo, coalition support was even more critical to the legitimacy of force because there had been no attempt to secure UN Security Council approval. But maintaining this support among nineteen nations proved immensely difficult. Some like Greece had long-standing religious and economic ties to the enemy. Others, like Italy, had few direct ties, but they were on the firing line. Hungary joined NATO only to find itself at war with its next-door neighbor, and with a substantial number of its native language speakers – the Hungarians of Voivodina – a potential hostage in Milosevic's hands. Another NATO partner, France, had the memory of an alliance with Serbia, going back to World War I, and believed that this entitled it to a separate margin of maneuver on both diplomatic and military fronts. The coalition presented itself as a united front: in reality, nineteen nations with very different agendas and traditions unwillingly went to war under American orders.

The operation was presented to the public as a display of alliance cohesion. In reality, the Americans did most of the fighting. According to Anthony Cordesman's careful study for the Center for Strategic and International Studies in Washington, the US flew over 60 percent of all sorties, over 80 percent of the strike sorties, over 90 percent of the advanced intelligence and reconnaissance missions, over 90 percent of the electronic warfare missions and fired over 80 percent of the precision guided weapons and over 95 percent of the Cruise missiles.[59] It is not simply that the Americans dominated the operational side of the mission; they also kept their NATO allies excluded from all targeting decisions involving American aircraft, and denied them intelligence for all targets struck by American missiles or planes.

At the political level, the alliance held together. At the military level, alliance cohesion was a myth. Right through the campaign, each nation reserved the right to refuse to send its air crews into operations which had not received explicit sanction from its national governments and its targeting lawyers. The British, for example, believed that the bombing of the Serbian TV and the power grid constituted potential violations of the Geneva Conventions, and that the adverse diplomatic and political consequences of these strikes outweighed their military advantages.[60] So no British pilots took part. Similarly, the French government refused to take part in strikes against Belgrade bridges and managed to dissuade other allies from taking them all down.[61]

When a Russian tank column, attached to the NATO stabilization force in Bosnia, raced to Pristina airport in June 1999, and Wesley Clark, Supreme Commander, Europe, ordered General Michael Jackson, the British Commander of NATO troops in Kosovo to prevent the Russians occupying the airport, Jackson refused, going to his political superiors in London to secure authorization to refuse a direct command.[62] Despite the appearance of a single chain of command within NATO, national military officers possessed the right to appeal orders to their own national leadership.

The alliance held together, but it did so by becoming virtual. Public displays of political unity were a façade, concealing substantive disagreements over targeting, tactics, as well as diplomatic strategy. Appearance and reality diverged, and maintaining the illusion of unity was crucial to the military outcome. Milosevic knew that if he could crack the image of alliance cohesion, he could break support for the war and stop the NATO machine. Hence, concealment of these disputes became an essential element of the propaganda war. If voters in the nineteen NATO countries had had any idea just how divided the alliance actually was – General Clark calling for a ground option, the Pentagon dissenting; the American air commanders demanding to 'go downtown', i.e. to Belgrade, the French flatly refusing; the Germans seriously considering Russian peace initiatives, the British and Americans appalled by their apparent willingness to appease Milosevic – their support would have begun to crumble. As it was, leaks about this disunity were becoming apparent by the end of the campaign. One reason why the alliance may have decided to conclude operations in early June and settle for less than total victory was that its leadership sensed 'alliance cohesion' – even of this virtual kind – could not be maintained much longer.

10. *Virtual Victory*

Virtual war proceeds to virtual victory. Since the means employed are limited, the ends achieved are equally constrained: not unconditional surrender, regime change or destruction of the war-making capacity of the other side, only an ambiguous 'end state'. Instead of Serb surrender in Kosovo, the NATO alliance contented itself with a 'military technical agreement' which, as its name implies, specified the terms and timing of Serbian withdrawal and the entry of NATO troops, but left entirely undefined the juridical status of the territory over which the war was fought.

Why do virtual wars end so ambiguously? Nations impose unconditional surrender on their enemies only when they have suffered some harm – death of their citizens, loss of their territory – which seems to require a fight to the death. Wars fought in the name of the human rights of other nation's national minorities are bound to be self-limiting. We fight for victory and for unconditional surrender only when we are fighting for ourselves.

Had we suffered casualties in Kosovo we might have been both less tender about inflicting collateral damage on their civilians and less circumspect about victory. Had our soldiers died we might well have pressed on for something more robust than a military-technical agreement.

But why – in Iraq and again in Kosovo – did we shrink before the idea of changing a hated regime? We demonized both Saddam Hussein and Milosevic and yet left them in place. This extraordinary gap between rhetoric and performance once again reflects a conflict in our own interests: between human rights and stability. A rogue state is judged to be better than no state at all. A Serbia and an Iraq that remain intact, under despotic leadership, are both preferred to societies dissolving into civil war. And since – a further contradiction – Western nations believe in self-determination, they are unwilling to occupy these defeated states and rebuild them from the bottom up in a properly imperial fashion. Woodrow Wilson at Versailles bequeathed to the century the idea of self-determination; and once uttered, a commitment to self-determination makes for imperialists with bad consciences. And bad consciences make for limited goals when it comes to war.

Conscience in this instance is allied with interest – for who would not prefer to be an imperial arbiter of a region without the burdens of actual occupation? But a world in which richer nations are unwilling – as a matter of principle and calculation – to bring order to poorer nations is of necessity a less stable world. America has certainly hoped to enjoy hegemony on the cheap, to profit from the collapse of its Cold War antagonist, without having to invest in the post-Cold War peace. But the reality of the post-Cold War world has not been the irresistible advance of liberal democracy and free markets, but chaos: the collapse of the state structure of three regions – the Balkans, the Caucasus and the Great Lakes region of Africa – into endemic civil war. Liberal democracies that are unwilling to repair collapsed states, to create democracy where none existed, and to remain on guard until the institutions are self-sustaining and self-reproducing, must inevitably discover that virtual victory is a poor substitute for the real thing.

11. Waiting for the Barbarians

Virtual wars fought in the name of virtually mobilized but largely passive electorates for the sake of virtual victories are not likely to produce long-lasting advantages to those who wage them. Nor are the advantages which leadership in the revolution in military affairs confers on the United States likely to be permanent. The technologies involved are neither abstruse nor expensive, and in time, America will lose its monopoly over them.[63] There is a contradiction between American national security which directs US policy towards safeguarding its monopoly and American commitment to free trade and open markets which favours exporting military technology worldwide. Over the long term, the contradiction is likely to be resolved in favor of American capitalism. If American companies wish to export encryption, super-computers and weapons technologies to other nations, national security considerations will not be allowed to stand in their way and as they do so, American technological monopolies will be lost. Other nations will begin to produce and deploy long-range precision guided weapons and as they do so America will become more vulnerable to attack. In response, it will have to develop missile defense systems to protect the continental United States.

In the long term, American military advantage will be whittled away by friend and foe alike, forcing a constant effort by American military services to conserve some useable competitive advantage. America can control its friends, the NATO allies, essentially by tying these European defense forces into the structure of American technology in such a way that they will have no incentive to develop non-complementary systems. America can keep European defense spending at non-competitive levels essentially by continuing to guarantee European security. This may be a relatively cheap way of bribing potential competitors out of the defense technology race. But America will have a more difficult time with genuine competitors like Russia or China. Already in Chechnya, the Russian army is seeking to avenge its defeat at the hands of Chechen rebels in 1996 by adopting the standoff tactics of aerial bombardment used by the Americans and then by taking precisely those risks with ground troops to which American commanders seem so averse. In the longer term, the Russian military will seek parity in precision-guided munitions, and any Russian leader will be bound, by considerations of national interest, to find the funding to make this possible. There is no reason to suppose that the American monopoly of precision weaponry will endure.

As for rogue states, they are likely to take the advice proffered by the Indian general who remarked after the Gulf War that its chief lesson was 'Never fight the Americans without nuclear weapons.'[64] While the Indian government has no desire to fight the Americans it has certainly followed its

211

general's advice, acquiring a nuclear capability in order to deter the Pakistanis and the Chinese. The revolution in conventional weaponry is thus accelerating proliferation in the nuclear and the chemical and biological fields. Saddam Hussein sought to acquire a stock of chemical and nerve agents precisely because the Gulf War had taught him that his armed forces stood no chance against American and Israeli air power. Chemical and biological weapons are vile and indiscriminate in their effects, but that is precisely why they offer the most effective deterrent against American precision weapons systems. American missile defense systems can be counted on to knock down the precision weapons of rogue states; but there is no possible deterrent, other than unremitting vigilance, against the release of small but lethal doses of chemical or biological toxins against American citizens.

Technological superiority is thus not a guarantee of national security and there is no reason to believe that zero-casualty, zero-risk, zero-defect warfare will actually result in a safer world, or even a world safer just for Americans.

Virtual war, therefore, is a dangerous illusion. It has emerged because it promises to restore war to its place as the continuation of politics by other means. But war should always remain the instrument of very last resort. This is not to imply that we can always avoid its use. War endures because human interests, values and commitments are occasionally irreconcilable. Where these conflicts cannot be conciliated, war remains the ultimate arbiter of human disagreements. The conflict in Kosovo was radical and unbridgeable: between a state bent on maintaining control of a territory by any means whatever and an ethnic majority determined to fight for self-determination. Central commitments of the world since Auschwitz, since the

Universal Declaration of Human Rights – that nation states do not have the right to massacre their citizens – would have meant nothing if we had not been prepared to use force in their defense. We should be prepared to do so in the future, and with determination. War must always be the very last instrument of policy – but when the sword is raised, it must be used to strike decisively, for only decisive force yields the results which can justify its use in the first place.

Having said this much for war – and for the necessity of war in defense of human rights – we need to reflect on the potential for self-righteous irrationality which lies hidden in abstractions like human rights. Those who supported the Kosovo war must face up to the unintended effects of moralizing the use of violence. For high-flown abstractions carry an inherent justification of everything done in their name. What is to prevent moral abstractions like human rights from inducing an absolutist frame of mind which, in defining all human rights violators as barbarians, legitimizes barbarism?

It will be said that human rights language cannot be perverted to such ends. While the language of the nation is particularistic – dividing human beings into us and them – human rights is universal. In theory, it will not lend itself to dividing human beings into higher and lower, superior and inferior, civilized and barbarian. Yet something very like a distinction between superior and inferior has been at work in the demonization of human rights violators. We say the demonization applies only to rulers, but imperceptibly, the ruled are also tainted by our moral scorn. Indeed the immense moral prestige which has accrued to human rights makes it a seductive, even unanswerable justification for the use of force. The language of human rights easily lends itself to the invention of a virtual moral world peopled by demonized enemies and rogue states, facing virtuous allies and noble armies. The more distant we are the easier it is to succumb to the lure of these fictions. As one World War II veteran once remarked, 'a civilian far removed from the battle area is nearly certain to be more bloodthirsty than the front-line soldier.' Those who support military intervention in defense of human rights need to back up their abstract commitments with devout attention to the question of whether, by intervening, we end up destroying what we tried to save.

Devout attention to the real is a form of virtue, as the philosopher Hannah Arendt noted in a short introduction she wrote in 1966 to an extraordinary memoir by J. Glenn Gray about his years fighting as an intelligence officer in Italy, Germany and France during World War II. Arendt observed that 'both abstract notions and abstract emotions are not merely false to what actually happens but are viciously interconnected.' For – and here she quotes Glenn Gray himself – 'abstract thinking is strictly comparable to the inhumanity of abstract emotions'.[65] Moral danger, this warrior warns us, lies in failing to ask ourselves clearly enough whether our moral emotions are real, whether they authentically belong to us and accurately respond to a situation – an abuse, a crime, a catastrophe – as it really is.

We live our lives in language and thus in representation. We always see through a glass darkly, never face to face. Yet even if the real is hidden, it exists and by inference and patient study, we can make out its shape. Only the most devoted attention to what is real can help us to make judgments and take actions which are both responsible and efficacious. Virtual reality is seductive. We see ourselves as noble warriors and our enemies as despicable tyrants. We see war as a surgical scalpel and not a bloodstained sword. In so doing we mis-describe ourselves as we mis-describe the instruments of death. We need to stay away from such fables of self-righteous invulnerability. Only then can we get our hands dirty. Only then can we do what is right.

NOTES

"World War III? Hmm. O.K., but , remember, nobody gets hurt."

Notes

Introduction

1 Wesley Clark, 'Press Briefing on the Kosovo Strike Assessment', (Brussels, NATO Headquarters, September 16, 1999).

2 Michael Ignatieff, *Blood and Belonging: Journeys into the New Nationalism* (London: Chatto & Windus, 1993; New York: Farrar Straus, 1993); *The Warrior's Honor: Ethnic War and the Modern Conscience* (London: Chatto & Windus, 1998; New York: Metropolitan Books, 1998).

The War of Words: A Dialogue on Intervention

1 See my *Isaiah Berlin: A Life*, (London: Chatto & Windus, 1998; New York: Metropolitan Books, 1998); also Isaiah Berlin, 'Two Concepts of Liberty' in Henry Hardy (ed.) *The Proper Study of Mankind*, (London: Chatto & Windus, 1997), 197, 242.

2   Tony Blair 'Speech to the Economic Club of Chicago, 22 April 1999'.

3   Robert Skidelsky, *John Maynard Keynes*, 2 vols. (London: Macmillan, 1992).

Justice and Revenge

1   On the draft statute of the International Criminal Court, see Geoffrey Robertson, *Crimes Against Humanity, The Struggle for Global Justice* (London: Allen Lane, 1999) Ch.9.

Enemies and friends

1   Michael Ignatieff, 'A Post-Modern War' in *Time*, April 12, 1999.

2   Quoted from Aleksa Djilas, 'A Profile of Slobodan Milosevic', *Foreign Affairs.*, Summer 1993.

3   I discuss Milovan Djilas' career in greater detail in 'Prophet in the Ruins,' *New York Review of Books*, March 4, 1999; also see Milovan Djilas, *Fall of the New Class: A History of Communism's Self-Destruction*, (New York: Knopf, 1998).

4   Aleksa Djilas, *The Contested Country: Yugoslav Unity and Communist Revolution, 1919-1993*, (Cambridge: Harvard University Press, 1991).

5   Aleksa Djilas, 'The Yugoslav Tragedy', *Prospect*, October, 1995.

Virtual War

1   Paul W. Kahn, 'War and Sacrifice in Kosovo,' *Philosophy and Public Policy*, 19, Spring/Summer 1999. See also Michael Walzer 'Kosovo,' *Dissent*, Summer 1999.

2   James Mayall (ed.), *The New Interventionism, 1991–4* (Cambridge: University Press, 1996); Christopher Greenwood, 'International Law, Just War and the Conduct of Modern Military Operations' in 'Military Ethics', RIIA Seminar, Chatham House,

London, 1998.

3 Quoted in Charles J. Dunlap, 'Technology: Recomplicating Moral Life for the Nation's Defenders' in *Parameters* Autumn 1999, 24–53.

4 Sun Tzu, *The Art of War*, foreword by Norman Stone (London, Wordsworth Editions, 1990), p. 105.

5 BBC *Future War* Interview, July 1999, George Freedman, Stratfor Inc. Austin, Texas. See also J.W. Gibson, *The Perfect War: Technowar in Vietnam* (Boston: Atlantic Monthly Press, 1986); Mark Clodfelter, *The Limits of Air Power: The American Bombing of North Vietnam* (New York: Free Press, 1989).

6 Lawrence Freedman, 'The Revolution in Strategic Affairs,' Adelphi Paper 31, London, IISS, 1998.

7 Andrew Marshall Interview for BBC Television's *Future War* project, July 1999, Washington.

8 Makhmut Gareev, *If War Comes Tomorrow: The Contours of Future Armed Conflict*, (London, Cass, 1998); Mary Fitzgerald, *The New Revolution in Russian Military Affairs*, (London, RUSI, 1994).

9 Kenneth Adelman, 'The Real Ronald Reagan', *Wall Street Journal*, September 1999.

10 Anthony Cordesman, 'The Lessons and Non-Lessons of the Air and Missile War in Kosovo', (Washington: Center for Strategic and International Studies, 1999).

11 Joanna Bourke, *An Intimate History of Killing: Face to Face Killing in 20th Century Warfare* (London, Granta, 1999), 6.

12 W. A. Owens, 'The Emerging System of Systems' in *Proceedings*, Naval War College, May 1995, 35–9.

13 Martin Shaw, *Post-Military Society* (London, Polity, 1991), 146.

14 Interview Gen. Andrew Sullivan, BBC *Future War* project, July 199.

15 Tom Ricks, 'Sticking to their Guns,' *Wall Street Journal*, Oct. 13, 1999.

16 Interview General Paul K. Van Riper, US Marines, BBC *Future War* project, July 1999.

17 Interview Norman Schwarzkopf, BBC *Future War* project, March 1999.

18 Joel Garreau, 'Reboot Camp: As War Looms, the Marines Test New Networks of Comrades,' *Washington Post*, March 24, 1999; Joel Garreau, 'Point Men for a Revolution: Can the Marines Survive a Shift from Hierarchies to Networks,' *Washington Post*, March 6, 1999.

19 Robert F. Scales, *Future War: Anthology* (Carlisle Barracks, Pennsylvania: U.S. Army War College, 1999).

20 This is based on discussion with Col. Douglas McGregor, SHAPE, Mons, Belgium, 1999; see also Douglas McGregor, 'Command and Control for Joint Strategic Actions,' *Joint Force Quarterly*, 20, December 1999.

21 For a discussion of state power and globalization which avoids these clichés, see David Held, Anthony McGrew, David Goldblatt and Jonathan Perraton, *Global Transformations: Politics, Economics and Culture* (London: Polity Press, 1999), especially 436–444.

22 Bypassing Congress is not a new phenomenon. Since Truman's initiation of war in Korea through to President Johnson's Gulf of Tonkin Resolution, American Presidents have circumvented the war-declaring powers of the US Congress. See F.D. Wormuth, *To Chain the Dog of War* (Chicago, University of Illinois Press, 1989); Brian Hallet, *The Lost Art of Declaring War* (Urbana, University of Illinois Press, 1998); J.H. Ely, *War and Responsibility* (Princeton, Princeton University Press, 1993).

23 Anthony Cordesman, 'Lessons and Non-lessons, executive summary', 9.

24 David Rieff, *Slaughterhouse: Bosnia and the Failure of the West* (New York, Simon and Schuster, 1995); on Clinton policy in 1992–3, see Sidney Blumenthal, 'Lonesome Hawk,' *The New Yorker*, May 31, 1993.

25 Sixty-one percent of Americans, as compared to 37 percent of Frenchmen and 47 percent of British citizens believe their country should not get involved in foreign wars. See ICRC 'People on War: Country Report: France, United Kingdom, United States,' [ICRC, Geneva, 1999, p. 1.]

26 The UN Secretary General, Kofi Annan, has led the debate on Security Council ratification of intervention. See Kofi Annan, 'Address to the United Nations General Assembly,' New York, September 20, 1999.

27 Samuel Huntington, *The Soldier and the State* (Cambridge, Mass., Belknap, 1957), ch 2.

28 On war and masculinity, George L. Mosse, *The Image of Man: The Creation of Modern Masculinity* (New York, Oxford University Press, 1996).

29 Donald Sassoon, *One Hundred Years of Socialism* (London, HarperCollins, 1996), ch. 4.

30 Jay Winter, *Sites of Memory, Sites of Mourning: The Great War in European Cultural History* (Cambridge, University Press, 1995); Donovan Webster, *Aftermath: The Remnants of War* (New York, Pantheon, 1996).

31 Edward Luttwak, 'Towards Post-Heroic Warfare,' *Foreign Affairs*, May–June, 1995.

32 'La Nouvelle Conscription des jeunes français se met en place,' *Le Monde*, October 1, 1998.

33 H.R. McMaster, *Dereliction of Duty: Lyndon Johnson, Robert McNamara, the Joint Chiefs of Staff and the Lies that Led to Vietnam* (New York, HarperCollins, 1997); Gloria Emerson,

Winners and Losers (New York, Harvest Books, 1976).

34 On the role of television in ending the war in Vietnam see the essays in '1968' a special issue of *Media Studies Journal*, (12,3, Fall 1998).

35 Tom Ricks, 'The Widening Gap Between the Military and Society,' *The Atlantic Monthly*, July 1997; see also Tom Ricks, *Making the Corps* (New York, Touchstone 1997).

36 Peter Feaver and Richard Kohn, 'Project on the Gap Between the Military and Civilian Society,' *Digest of Findings and Studies*, (Chapel Hill, NC, Triangle Institute for Security Studies, 1999).

37 *New York Times*, September 1999.

38 Tom Ricks, 'Sticking to its Guns,' *Wall Street Journal*, Oct. 13, 1999, Chart, p. 33.

39 Seymour Hersh, 'The Intelligence Gap: How the Digital Age Left Our Spies out in the Cold,' *The New Yorker*, December 6, 1999.

40 Jacques Gansler Interview for BBC Television's *Future War* July 1999; see also J. Gansler, 'Changes in Technology and Warfare,' IISS Conference Paper, Oxford, September 1998.

41 *Time*, November 8, 1999.

42 Mark Bowden, *Blackhawk Down* (New York: Atlantic Monthly Press, 1999).

43 Jessica Stern, *The Ultimate Terrorists* (Cambridge, Mass., Harvard University Press, 1999).

44 James Buchan, 'Inside Iraq,' *Granta Magazine*, 67, Autumn 1999; Christophe Girod, *Tempête sur le Desert* (Paris, Bruylant, 1995), 138–140.

45 I visited Halabja in 1993. See Michael Ignatieff, *Blood and Belonging: Journeys into the New Nationalism*, (London, Vintage, 1993, 149–51).

46 Telephone Interview by Michael Ignatieff with Alastair Campbell, Prime Minister's Press Secretary, July 1999.

47 Julian Manyon, *The Spectator*, May 1999. Manyon was the ITN correspondent in Belgrade who was on the scene soon after the TV station attack.

48 Steven Keeva, 'Lawyers in the War Room,' *American Bar Association Journal*, December 1991; Girod, *Tempête sur le Desert*, 139; 'The Role of the Law of War' in *Conduct of the Persian Gulf Conflict*, US Department of Defense Report to the US Congress, April 1992. Terrie M. Gent, 'The Role of Judge Advocates in a Joint Air Operations Center,' *Air Chronicles*, Spring 1999.

49 Interview with Col. Tony Montgomery, JAG, EUCOM, Frankfurt, Germany, November 1999, BBC Television *Future War* project.

50 For an unconvincing attempt to show that the Chinese embassy strike was deliberate, see John Sweeney and Jens Holsoe, 'NATO bombed Chinese deliberately', the *Observer*, 17 October 1999.

51 Anthony Cordesman, 'Lessons and Non-Lessons of the Air and Missile War in Kosovo', (Washington, CSIS, 1999).

52 Colonel Douglas McGregor, private communication, October 1999.

53 C. J. Dunlap, 'Technology: Recomplicating the Moral Life for the Nation's Defenders,' *Parameters*, Autumn 1999.

54 I have explored these issues further in 'The Ingenuity of Barbarians,' *Red Cross-Red Crescent Magazine*, (Geneva, ICRC, September 1999).

55 See Michael Ignatieff, 'Human Rights: The mid-life Crisis', *New York Review of Books*, May 20, 1999; Geoffrey Robertson, *Crimes Against Humanity: The Struggle for Global Justice* (London, Allen Lane, 1999); A.H. Robertson and J.G. Merrills, *Human Rights in the World* (Manchester, Manchester University Press, 1996).

56 Noam Chomsky, *The New Military Humanism: Lessons from Kosovo* (Vancouver, B.C., 1999).

57 Robert C. Owen, 'The Balkans Air Campaign Study, Parts 1 and 2,' *Airpower Journal*, Summer and Fall 1997.

58 Elizabeth Becker, 'Military Leaders Tell Congress of NATO Errors in Kosovo,' *New York Times*, October 15, 1999; see also Joint Statement of William S. Cohen and Henry H. Shelton to the Senate Armed Services Committee Hearing on Kosovo After-Action Review, October 14, 1999.

59 Anthony Cordesman, 'Lessons and Non-Lessons: Executive Summary', 9.

60 My source here – who wishes to remain anonymous – is a military lawyer attached to the Royal Air Force.

61 President Chirac, interview by Jacques Isnard, *Le Monde*, June 1999.

62 Elizabeth Becker, 'US General Was Overruled in Kosovo,' *New York Times*, September 10, 1999.

63 Robert H. Scales, *Future Warfare: Anthology*, p. 35.

64 Quoted in Lawrence Freedman, 'The Revolution in Strategic Affairs,' Adelphi Paper, 318, IISS, London, 1998, 45.

65 J. Glenn Gray, *The Warriors: Reflections on Men in Battle*, introduction by Hannah Arendt (University of Nebraska Press, 1998), viii–ix.

Further Reading

Kosovo: *Context and Background*

Brzezinski, Zbigniew, 'Why Milosevic Cracked,' *Prospect Magazine*, November 1999.

Burg, Steven L. and Shoup Paul S., *The War in Bosnia-Herzegovina: Ethnic Conflict and International Intervention* (New York: M.E. Sharpe, 1999).

Fromkin, David, *Kosovo Crossing* (New York: Free Press, 1999).

Garton Ash, Timothy, *History of the Present* (London: Penguin, 1999).

Glenny, Misha, *The Balkans, 1804–1999* (London: Granta Books, 1999).

Holbrooke, Richard, *To End a War* (New York: Random House, 1998).

Human Rights Watch, *Human Rights Abuses in Kosovo* (New York: Human Rights Watch, 1993)

Human Rights Watch, *Humanitarian Law Violations in Kosovo* (New York: Human Rights Watch, 1998)

Human Rights Watch, *A Week of Terror in Drenica: Humanitarian Law Violations in Kosovo* (New York: Human Rights Watch, 1999)

Judah, Tim, *The Serbs: History, Myth and the Destruction of Yugoslavia* (New Haven: Yale University Press, 1997).

Judah, Tim, 'Inside the KLA' *New York Review of Books*, June 10, 1999.

Malcolm, Noel, *Kosovo: A Short History* (London: Macmillan, 1998).

Mandelbaum, Michael, 'A Perfect Failure,' *Foreign Affairs*, September–October 1999.

Silber, Laura and Little, Alan, *The Death of Yugoslavia* (London: Penguin, 1995).

Woodward, Susan, *The Balkan Tragedy* (London, Brookings, 1995).

The Right to Intervene

Annan, Kofi, 'Address to the UN Commission on Human Rights,' Geneva, April 7, 1999.

Annan, Kofi, 'Address to the Centennial of the First International Peace Conference,' The Hague, May 18, 1999.

Annan, Kofi, 'Address to the United Nations General Assembly,' New York, September 20, 1999.

Callahan, David, *Unwinnable Wars: American Power and Ethnic Conflict* (New York: Hill and Wang, 1997).

Chomsky, Noam, *The New Military Humanism: Lessons from Kosovo* (Vancouver: New Star Books, 1999).

Mayall, James, (ed.), *The New Interventionism, 1991–1994* (Cambridge: Cambridge University Press, 1996).

Laws of War

Dunlap, Charles J., 'Technology: Recomplicating Moral Life for the Nation's Defenders,' *Parameters: US Army War College Quarterly*, Autumn 1999, 24–53.

Ely, J.H., *War and Responsibility: Constitutional Lessons of Vietnam and its Aftermath* (Princeton: Princeton University Press, 1993).

Gent, Terrie M., 'The Role of Judge Advocates in a Joint Air Operations Center,' *Air Chronicles*, Spring 1999.

Girod, Christophe, *Tempête sur le Desert: Le Comité International de la Croix-Rouge et La Guerre du Golfe, 1990–1* (Paris: Bruylant, 1995).

Greenwood, Christopher, 'International Law and the Conduct of War,' IISS Annual Conference, Oxford, 1998.

Greenwood, Christopher, 'Law and the Conduct of Military Operations,' Military Ethics Seminar, Chatham House, RIIA, London, 1998.

Hallet, Brien, *The Lost Art of Declaring War* (Urbana: University of Illinois Press, 1998).

International Committee of the Red Cross, 'People on War: Country Report – France, United Kingdom, United States,' Report by Greenberg Research, (Geneva: ICRC, 1999).

International Committee of the Red Cross, 'People on War: Country Report – Russian Federation,' (Geneva: ICRC, 1999).

Wormuth, F.D., and Firmage, E.B., *To Chain the Dog of War: The War Power of Congress in History and Law*, Second edition (Chicago: University of Illinois Press, 1989).

Zero Casualty War

Garwin, Richard L. and Winfield, M. W., *Nonlethal Tech-*

nologies: Progress and Prospect, Independent Task Force Report (New York: Council on Foreign Relations, 1999).

Kahn, Paul W., 'War and Sacrifice in Kosovo,' *Philosophy and Public Policy*, 19, Spring–Summer 1999.

Luttwak, Edward N., 'Towards Post-Heroic Warfare', *Foreign Affairs*, May–June 1995.

Tucker, David, 'Fighting Barbarians' in *Parameters*, Summer 1998, 69–79.

Walzer, Michael, 'Kosovo,' *Dissent*, Summer 1999.

The Revolution in Military Affairs

Blaker, James R., 'Understanding the Revolution in Military Affairs' (Washington: Progressive Policy Institute, 1997).

Blaker, James R., 'Revolutions in Military Affairs: Why the Critique?,' *NSSQ*, Winter 1999, 83–91.

Fitzgerald, Mary, *The New Revolution in Russian Military Affairs* (London: Royal United Services Institute for Defence Studies, 1994).

Freedman, Lawrence, *The Revolution in Strategic Affairs* (London: International Institute for Strategic Studies, Adelphi Paper 318, 1998).

Gareev, Makhmut, *If War Comes Tomorrow? The Contours of Future Armed Conflict* (London: Frank Cass, 1995).

Heisbourg, François, *The Future of Warfare* (London: Orion, 1997).

Laird, R.F. and Mey, H.H., *The Revolution in Military Affairs* (Washington: Institute for National Strategic Studies, 1999).

Lind, William et al., 'The Changing Face of War: Into the Fourth Generation,' *Marine Corps Gazette*, October 1989.

Lind, William et al., 'Fourth Generation Warfare: Another Look,' *Marine Corps Gazette*, December 1994.

Marshall, Andrew A., 'Revolutions in Military Affairs: Testimony Before the Senate Armed Services Committee,' May 5, 1995.

Owens, William A., 'The Emerging System of Systems,' *Proceedings*, May 1995, 35–9.

Scales, Robert H., *Future Warfare: Anthology* (Carlisle Barracks, Pennsylvania: US Army War College, 1999)

Sullivan, Brian R., 'The Future Nature of Conflict: A Critique of "The American Revolution in Military Affairs" in the Era of Jointery,' *Defense Analysis*, 14: 2, 1998.

Toffler, Alvin and Toffler, Heidi, *War and Anti-War: Survival at the Dawn of the Twenty-first Century* (Boston: Little Brown, 1993).

Changing Face of War

Adams, James, *The Next World War: The Warriors and Weapons of the New Battlefields in Cyberspace* (London: Hutchinson, 1998).

Arquilla, John and Ronfeldt, David, 'Cyberwar is Coming,' *Comparative Strategy*, 12, 141–65, 1993.

Boutwell, Jeffrey and Klare, Michael T., (eds.), *Light Weapons and Civil Conflict: Controlling the Tools of Conflict* (New York: Rowman and Littlefield, 1999).

Bowden, Mark, *Blackhawk Down* (New York: Atlantic Monthly Press, 1999).

Coker, Christopher, *War and the Twentieth Century: The Impact of War on the Modern Consciousness* (London: Brasseys, 1994).

De Landa, Manuel, *War in the Age of Intelligent Machines* (New York: Swerve, 1991).

Delmas, Philippe, *The Rosy Future of War* (New York: The Free

Press, 1995).

Der Derian, James, 'Battlefield of Tomorrow,' *Wired* (July 1999).

Der Derian, James, 'The Virtualization of Violence and the Disappearance of War,' *Cultural Values* (October 1997).

Dixon, Norman, *On the Psychology of Military Incompetence* (London: Pimlico, 1994).

MacGregor, Douglas, *Breaking the Phalanx: A New Design for Landpower in the Twenty-first Century* (Westport: Praeger, 1997).

Doyle, Michael W., *Ways of War and Peace* (New York: Norton, 1997).

Economist, 'Defence Technology' in *Going Digital: How New Technology is Changing our Lives* (London, 1996).

Economist, 'The Future of Warfare,' March 8, 1997.

Economist, 'Other People's Wars,' July 31, 1999.

Flamm, Kenneth, 'Defence Industry and the Means of War,' IISS Annual Conference, Oxford, 1998.

Goure, Daniel and Szara, Christopher M., *Air and Space Power in the New Millennium* (Washington D.C., Center for Strategic and International Studies, 1997).

Gray, Chris Hables, *Post-Modern War: The New Politics of Conflict* (New York: The Guilford Press, 1997).

Gray, J. Glenn, *The Warriors: Reflections on Men in Battle*, introduction by Hannah Arendt (London: University of Nebraska Press, 1970, 1998).

Howard, Michael, 'When are Wars Decisive?' IISS Annual Conference, Oxford, 1998.

Hughes, Patrick M., 'Global Threats and Challenges: The Decades Ahead,' Statement for the Senate Select Committee on Intelligence, January 28, 1998, January 29, 1999.

Huntington, Samuel P., *The Soldier and the State: The Theory and Politics of Civil-Military Relations* (Cambridge, Mass.: Belknap, 1958).

Kaldor, Mary, *New and Old Wars: Organized Violence in a Global Era* (London: Polity, 1999).

Luttwak, Edward N., 'Give War a Chance,' *Foreign Affairs*, July/August 1999.

Mandelbaum, Michael, 'Is Major War Obsolete?' IISS Annual Conference, Oxford, 1998.

McMaster, H.R., *Dereliction of Duty: Lyndon Johnson, Robert McNamara, the Joint Chiefs of Staff and the Lies that Led to Vietnam* (New York: HarperCollins, 1997).

Minear, Larry et al., *The News Media, Civil War and Humanitarian Action* (Boulder: Rienner, 1994).

Murray, Williamson, 'Clausewitz Out, Computer In,' *The National Interest*, Summer, 1997.

Murray, Williamson, 'Preparing to Lose the Next War,' *Strategic Review*, Spring 1998.

Murray, Williamson, 'Air War in the Gulf: The Limits of Air Power,' *Strategic Review*, Winter 1998.

Murray, Williamson, 'Military Culture Does Matter,' *Strategic Review*, Spring 1999.

Owen, Robert C., 'The Balkans Air Campaign,' *Air Chronicles*, Summer, Fall, 1997.

Peters, Ralph, *Fighting for the Future: Will America Triumph?* (Mechanicsburg, Pa.: Stackpole Books, 1999).

Ricks, Tom, *Making the Corps* (New York: Touchstone, 1998).

Shearer, David, 'Outsourcing War,' *Foreign Policy*, Fall 1998.

Stern, Jessica, *The Ultimate Terrorists* (Cambridge, Mass.: Harvard, 1999).

Tanter, Raymond, *Rogue Regimes: Terrorism and Proliferation* (New York: Saint Martins, 1998).

Tharoor, Shashi, 'The Future of Civil Conflict,' IISS Annual Conference, Oxford, 1998.

Thompson, Leroy, *Ragged War: The Story of Unconventional and Counter-Revolutionary Warfare* (London: Cassell, 1994).

Townsend, Charles, (ed.), *The Oxford Illustrated History of Modern War* (Oxford: Oxford University Press, 1997).

U.S. Marine Corps, *Warfighting: The U.S. Marine Corps Book of Strategy* (New York: Doubleday, 1994).

Van Riper, Paul K., 'A Concept for Future Military Operations on Urbanized Terrain,' (Washington: US Marine Corps, 1997).

Assessing the Kosovo Air War

Clark, Wesley K., 'Press Briefing on the NATO Kosovo Strike Assessment,' September 16, 1999.

Cohen, William S. and Shelton, H.H., 'Joint Statement to the Senate Armed Services Committee on Kosovo After-Action Review,' October 14, 1999.

Cordesman, Anthony H., 'The Lessons and Non-Lessons of the Air and Missile War in Kosovo,' Center for Strategic and International Studies, Washington, 1999.

Krepinevich, Andrew, 'Two Cheers for Air Power,' *Wall Street Journal*, June 11, 1999.

NATO Daily Press Briefings, March 24, 1999–June 11, 1999.

Ricks, Tom, 'Sticking to its Guns,' *Wall Street Journal*, October 13, 1999.

Spinney, F.C., 'Learning the Lessons We Want to Learn,' Proceedings of the U.S. Naval Institute, September 1999.

Interviews:

These interviews were conducted by me or by Rebecca Simor and Glyn Jones of BBC Television's *Future War* project, March–December 1999.

General Norman Schwarzkopf, retired US Army, Tampa, Florida.

William Lind, defense analyst, Washington.

General Patrick Hughes, Defense Intelligence Agency, Washington.

General Charles Krulak, Commander, United States Marines, Quantico, Virginia.

General Wesley Clark, SACEUR, Shape Headquarters, Mons, Belgium.

Jacques Gansler, Department of Defense Washington.

Andrew Marshall, Department of Defense, Washington.

Andrew Krupenevich, Office of Net Assessment, Department of Defense, Washington

General Paul K. Van Riper, US Marines Corps, Quantico.

General Gordon R. Sullivan, Chief of Staff, United States Army, 1991–5.

Additional Interviews Conducted by MI:

Alastair Campbell, Press Secretary to the Prime Minister, Downing Street, SW1

Colonel Douglas McGregor, Shape, Mons, Belgium.

General Dan Leaf, Aviano, Italy.

Useful Web Sites:

www.csis.org: center for strategic and international studies, washington.

www.fas.org: federation of american scientists

www.cfr.org: council on foreign relations, new york.

Acknowledgments

The author wishes to thank:

- Bill Buford and David Remnick of *The New Yorker*.
- Paul Wilson of *Saturday Night* magazine.
- David Goodhart, editor of *Prospect* magazine.
- Richard Holbrooke, Strobe Talbott, Wesley Clark, Christopher Hill, Louise Arbour, James Rubin, David Wright, David Scheffer, Douglas McGregor, Dan Leaf.
- Glyn Jones, Rebecca Simor, Diane Wales, Peter Ceresole and Robert Murphy of BBC Television's *Future War* project.
- Jenny Uglow of Chatto & Windus and Sara Bershtel at Metropolitan Books.
- Robert Skidelsky for consenting to a reprint of his part of our exchange on the Kosovo intervention, which first appeared in *Prospect* magazine, June 1999.
- Maya Petrushevskaya, Skopje, Macedonia.
- Aleksa Djilas, Belgrade.
- Paul Risley, ICTY, The Hague.
- Suzanna Zsohar, who makes everything possible.

Index

moral issues 161–4, *see
  also* human rights;
  'humanitarian
  intervention'
and national identity 185–6
nuclear 162, 164, 165,
  169, 187, 212
and RMA 164–77, 210–13
risk-free 162–3, 168–70,
  180–1
and socialism 185–6
Washington Post 116, 123

Whiteman Airforce Base,
  Missouri 103
Wilson, President Woodrow
  20, 209–11
World War, First 185, 186,
  193
World War, Second 143,
  145, 172, 186, 189, 193

Yeltsin, Boris 64, 86, 110
Yugoslavia 12, 127, 145–6,
  147, 148, 153, 154, 166